The Pinsent Masons Guide to

Insurance
Distribution

The Pinsent Masons Guide to
Insurance
Distribution

Editor: Andrew Long

Pinsent Masons

KOGAN
PAGE

London and Philadelphia

Publisher's note

Every possible effort has been made to ensure that the information contained in this book is accurate at the time of going to press, and the publishers and author cannot accept responsibility for any errors or omissions, however caused. No responsibility for loss or damage occasioned to any person acting, or refraining from action, as a result of the material in this publication can be accepted by the editor, the publisher or the author.

First published in Great Britain and the United States in 2007 by Kogan Page Limited

120 Pentonville Road
London N1 9JN
United Kingdom
www.kogan-page.co.uk

525 South 4th Street, #241
Philadelphia PA 19147
USA

© Pinsent Masons, 2007

ISBN-10 0 7494 4992 6
ISBN-13 978 0 7494 4992 6

British Library Cataloguing-in-Publication Data

A CIP record for this book is available from the British Library.

Library of Congress Cataloging-in-Publication Data

Pinsent Masons (Firm)
  The Pinsent Masons guide to insurance distribution / Pinsent Masons. – 1st ed.
      p. cm.
  Includes index.
  ISBN-13: 978-0-7494-4992-6
  ISBN-10: 0-7494-4992-6
1. Insurance law–Great Britain. 2. Insurance–Great Britain–State supervision. 3.
Insurance agents–Legal status, laws, etc.–Great Britain. 4. Financial Services
Authority (Great Britain)–Rules and practice. I. Title II. Title: Guide to
insurance distribution.
  KD1859.P56 2007
  346.41'086–dc22
                                                     2007008564

Typeset by Saxon Graphics Ltd, Derby
Printed and bound in Great Britain by MPG Books Ltd, Bodmin, Cornwall

Contents

Foreword   *viii*

Preface   *ix*

Acknowledgements   *x*

List of abbreviations   *xi*

1   Introduction   **1**

New technology   1

New distributors   2

New regulation   2

Key trends   3

The key questions   4

2   The regulatory framework for the insurance market   **8**

The background   8

The structure of FSA regulation   10

3   Obligations of a regulated firm   **20**

What's behind the rules?   20

What are the FSA Principles?   21

What's the relationship between the Principles and FSA Rules?   22

What are the practical implications of Principle 11?   23

What are the conditions for FSA authorisation?   23

What does the Handbook say about governance?   25

What are the general rules for employees?   27

4   The Insurance Conduct of Business Rules   **29**

Application and purpose (ICOB 1)   30

General rules (ICOB 2)   31

Financial promotion (ICOB 3)   33

Advising and selling standards (ICOB 4)   35
Product disclosure (ICOB 5)   39
Cancellation (ICOB 6)   40
Claims handling (ICOB 7)   42
Distance non-investment mediation contracts with retail
customers (ICOB 8)   45

5 The secondary insurance market   **48**
Who's in the market?   48
What's in it for insurers?   49
How does FSA regulation affect the secondary market?   50
What exclusions are available to secondary intermediaries?   50

6 Inadvertent breaches of the law   **60**
What is insurance?   60
What happens in borderline cases?   63

7 Principles of agency   **68**
What constitutes an agency in law?   68
What are the agent's rights and obligations?   69
What should contracts cover?   74

8 Pricing and remuneration   **80**
Pricing insurance products   80
Receiving and refunding premiums   83
Paying intermediaries   85

9 Funds held by intermediaries   **92**
What are the rules?   92
What do the rules mean?   94

10 Outsourcing   **104**
What is outsourcing?   104
What are the current trends?   105
How has outsourcing developed in the insurance business?   105
What are the regulatory and legal implications of insurance
outsourcing?   107
How should outsourcing contracts be drawn up?   110

11 Use of technology   **116**
Selling and servicing online   116
Use of personal data   122

12 Insurance and competition law — **131**
What are the rules? — 131
Do the rules apply to all agreements? — 132
How do the rules affect different types of agreements? — 135
How do we ensure compliance? — 141

13 Transfer of insurance business — **145**
Employment law: TUPE — 145
Part VII transfers — 154
Block transfer on renewal — 159

Index — *162*

Foreword

The general insurance industry is highly competitive and innovative. Recent years have seen rapid change, both in the range of products on offer and in the way they are distributed. Traditional direct and broker sales are now only a part of the landscape, as insurers have sought to find new markets and distribution channels. The secondary market in insurance has developed rapidly, as many commercial organisations, not traditionally focused on insurance, have recognised the value of participating in this important market.

The regulatory regime has also changed considerably. First, general insurance was brought under the supervision of the Financial Services Authority under the Financial Services and Markets Act 2000. In 2005 the activities of insurance intermediaries also became subject to FSA supervision, in compliance with the Insurance Mediation Directive. Self-regulation was left behind.

The increasing diversity and inventive spirit of its participants is good for both consumers and the industry. But that makes it even more important that standards of good business practice continue to be observed in the general insurance market. Market participants must be well informed about the legal and regulatory framework within which they must operate.

In-house lawyers and business executives alike need a sound understanding of the legal regime which governs their business activities, as well as the principles involved in successful contract drafting and negotiation. I therefore very much welcome this publication which aims to guide the way through an often complex set of statutory requirements and practical considerations. I hope that those who use this book will find it a valuable source of information and guidance.

Nick Starling
Director of General Insurance
The Association of British Insurers

Preface

In recent years, the way general insurance products are sold to the public has changed. Insurers and intermediaries have found more sophisticated sales channels, thanks in part to technological and business advances such as the internet and outsourcing. Branding has become crucial as affinity or corporate partnership arrangements have become commonplace, resulting in often quite complex contractual and agency relationships. The rules in, and made under, the Financial Services and Markets Act 2000 have further complicated the picture, especially since the FSA became the statutory regulator of insurance sales in January 2005.

Lawyers and business executives involved in putting together insurance distribution deals need a good understanding of the legal and regulatory framework within which the arrangements must be structured. From our extensive experience – we have handled literally hundreds of insurance distribution deals over the last few years – we have created what we hope is a readable and lively overview of the things to be considered in drafting and negotiating these contracts.

Acknowledgements

This book has been written by a cohort of expert authors from both the insurance team and across the firm. Chapters that have been written by or contain contributions from Pinsent Masons colleagues include:

- ICOB rules – Sarah Bond;
- secondary insurance market/inadvertent breaches of the law – Liz Johnson and Aaron Le Marquer;
- principles of agency – Tim Hoffman and Alexis Roberts;
- pricing and remuneration – Mark Neville and Martin Membery;
- funds held by intermediaries – Alexis Roberts;
- outsourcing – Angela Cha and Alexis Roberts;
- information technology – Louise Townsend and John Salmon;
- competition – Alan Davis;
- transferring insurance business – Matthew Griffith, Sarah Bond, Robert Mecrate-Butcher and Iain Sawers.

This project could not have been realised without the input and support from many others; there were extensive contributions from Geraint Evans, Susanna Corbishley and Liz Johnson. I thank my colleagues in the insurance team led by Tim Burton, particularly all those who wrestled with and produced the manuscript through its many drafts. But most of all I am indebted to Caroline Proud for her formidable sub-editing, helping to produce a text that I believe is clear and readable.

Andrew Long

List of abbreviations

ABI	Association of British Insurers	FOS	Financial Ombudsman Service
ABTA	Association of British Travel Agents	FSA	Financial Services Authority
APER	Statements of Principle and Code of Practice for Approved Persons	FSCS	Financial Services Compensation Scheme
AR	Appointed representative	FSMA	Financial Services and Markets Act 2000
ATM	automated teller machine	GISC	General Insurance Standards Council
BPO	business process outsourcing	HMRC	HM Revenue and Customs
CASS	Client Asset Sourcebook	ICOB	Insurance Conduct of Business
CC	Competition Commission	ICT	information and communications technology
CF	controlled function		
CIFAS	Credit Industry Fraud Avoidance Scheme	IDD	initial disclosure document
COB	Conduct of Business rules for investment contracts	INSPRU	Prudential Sourcebook for Insurers
DPA	Data Protection Act 1998	IP	intellectual property
DTI	Department of Trade and Industry	IPT	Insurance Premium Tax
EC	European Commission	IT	information technology
ECJ	European Court of Justice	MCCB	Mortgage Code Compliance Board
EEA	European Economic Area		
ETO	economic, technical or organisational	MCOB	Mortgage Conduct of Business
EU	European Union		
FIT	The Fit and Proper Test for Approved Persons	MMS	multimedia message service

OFT	Office of Fair Trading	SOX	Sarbanes–Oxley Act
OSIS	Origo Secure Internet Services	SUP	Supervision rules
		SYSC	Systems and Controls
PERG	Perimeter Guidance	T&C	training and competence rules
PPI	payment protection insurance		
		TUPE	The Transfer of Undertakings (Protection of Employment) Regulations
PRIN	Principles for Businesses		
PRU	Integrated Prudential Sourcebook		
RAO	Regulated Activities Order	VAT	Value Added Tax
		W3C	World Wide Web Consortium
SIB	Securities and Investment Board		
		WIPO	World Intellectual Property Organisation
SMS	short message service		

Introduction

The way general insurance products are sold to the public differs dramatically from, say, a generation ago. The insurance sector and the insurance market have been reshaped by:

- new technologies;
- new distributors; and
- most significantly of all, new regulation.

The purpose of this book is to help business executives and their lawyers make sense of the 'revolution'. In this chapter, we describe the key characteristics of the new environment, introducing the issues that will be covered in subsequent chapters.

New technology

An old-style insurance operation would involve one of two principal routes to market. Insurance companies would operate through their own direct sales forces, many of them calling door to door. Companies would have regional and local offices, but more often for administration of sales rather than the selling process itself. The alternative was through brokers, often positioned on (or above!) the high street, with connections and access to the main insurers as well as detailed knowledge of products and prices.

The older model was challenged by the rise of call centres; telesales offered a cheaper and potentially more effective alternative to the older distribution channels, whose costs continued to rise. More recently, the internet, websites and e-mails have transformed the landscape for both sales and marketing; 3G mobile phones and texting promise further developments.

Technology has revolutionised not just sales channels but also business processes. It has become more feasible (and arguably more fashionable) for insurance (and other) organisations to outsource parts of their operations. Geographical proximity to the customer is no longer essential; in the more extreme cases, activities are outsourced abroad, i.e. 'offshored'.

New distributors

Insurance is no longer sold just by insurance companies and mainstream insurance intermediaries. There is a third category of organisation: those for whom insurance is not their main business. Supermarkets and 'super-brands' have diversified through partnerships with insurance organisa-tions. (A major theme of this book is the interaction between insurance organisations, both insurers and intermediaries, and corporate partners and affinity organisations.)

New regulation

The biggest and most fundamental change in the regulation of the distri-bution of general insurance products took place in 2005. Although insurers were themselves regulated by statute before then, insurance distribution was subject to *self-regulation*. The principal body was the General Insurance Standards Council.

Since 2005, the distribution of insurance products has been governed by the Financial Services and Markets Act 2000 (FSMA). Statutory regulation of insurance distribution under FSMA is under the control of the Financial Services Authority (FSA). There are several important consequences:

- Most insurance intermediaries have to be FSA authorised.
- Unless an exemption applies, it is a **criminal offence** to carry out regu-lated insurance activities without authorisation.
- FSA-authorised organisations have to comply with FSA rules.

This has moved the goalposts for insurers, insurance intermediaries, corporate partners and affinity and other groups involved in insurance.

Structuring the transactions between such entities must now take into account both FSA rules and which parties are to be FSA authorised.

Key trends

Brands

Many older insurance company brands have simply disappeared. Brands that were based on a company's geographic location or its original connection with a particular source of business have declined in importance. Some of the older brands (particularly those based on the door-to-door model) lost their value through technological change; others have disappeared in the process of consolidation.

Perhaps paradoxically, alongside consolidation there has been segmentation. The number of major insurers has decreased in the past 15 years, largely due to mergers and takeovers; the number of major intermediaries has decreased for the same reason.

New brands have sprung up, often linked to technological change but frequently with a name that has no immediate connection with the insurer involved. (Sadly, it has to be recognised that customer brand loyalty – and trust – in some insurance brands is much less than in some other industries.)

New brands have new and different focuses. For example, some motor insurance brands have been based on the sex and/or location of the driver (interestingly, the geographical segmentation may be determined by the advertising methods – eg posters on the London Underground – rather than the location of the company's offices or sales force). Other brands have been built on a segmentation of the market by age; an alternative method of approaching the issue of age is by partnerships with brands that appeal to particular age groups.

Products

There have been two principal trends in relation to products. Firstly, more diverse products have been developed: it is now commonplace to see extended warranty insurance, pet insurance, insurance against boiler breakdown and income protection products. Secondly, such products are increasingly 'spin-offs' sold in the course of other business (see below).

Underlying the latter trend is basic economics. Many of these 'new' products yield comparatively small (per policy) premiums and are intended for a mass market. They can only be successfully (i.e. profitably) sold if the costs of distributing them are contained. Accordingly, there is considerable value, for the purposes of selling insurance, in having an accessible and extensive customer list and/or a respected and trusted brand.

Organisations with both a trusted brand and a large customer list can sell insurance more cheaply and more easily than insurers. An obvious example is that of the utility company; it can afford to offer low-yield products because it has thousands of customers already on its books with whom it has a longstanding relationship and regular contact.

Ways of buying

Consumers increasingly seek convenience and 'one stop' shopping. This means they're often receptive to opportunities to buy insurance at the same time as carrying out another transaction. Insurance is increasingly being 'bundled'. Extended warranty insurance is sold with household electrical goods, travel insurance with holidays, and income protection (against accident, sickness and unemployment) with mortgages or other loans and credit agreements. Similarly, professionals such as vets and dentists are well placed to sell insurance against the risk of needing to use their services.

Sometimes, multiple insurance sales may be possible. Car dealers could sell motor insurance, both to cover liabilities to others (third party) and accidental damage or theft (comprehensive). They may also be able to sell breakdown cover. If the customer is borrowing to buy the car, they could also sell income protection insurance against the risk of not being able to make the repayments. This is another example of how insurance distribution involves parties other than the conventional companies and intermediaries (usually, organisations that do not include the word insurance in their title).

The key questions

In this book, we endeavour to give answers to some of the key questions for modern insurance distribution and in particular for lawyers and business executives aiming to structure insurance deals.

What is the impact of regulation?

We deal with the basic structure of regulation and provide key information about the FSA, its Handbook and FSMA in Chapter 2. The chapter covers the insurance activities that fall within the FSA ambit – and those that fall outside it.

The consequences of being regulated are dealt with in Chapters 3 and 4. Chapter 3 outlines the general rules that are applied to regulated organisations. It contains information on the high-level FSA principles and rules and the consequences of breaching them.

The detailed rules for the distribution of general insurance products – the Insurance Conduct of Business (ICOB) rules – are dealt with in Chapter 4. ICOB is the key section of the FSA Handbook for general insurance distribution, containing the main body of rules and guidance on advertising, advising and selling, product disclosure, cancellation rights and procedures, and claims handling.

How are non-insurance organisations affected?

As indicated above, there is a thriving 'secondary' insurance market: the sale and distribution of insurance products increasingly involves organisations whose core business is something else.

Chapter 5 looks at the impact of regulation on these organisations, at the exclusions available to them and at some of the general principles for contracts between insurers and intermediaries. It explains why insurers use secondary intermediaries and includes an important section on appointed representatives – intermediaries that do not need to be authorised by the FSA provided someone takes responsibility for them.

What is regulated insurance and how is the law likely to decide borderline cases?

It is possible to enter into an arrangement that constitutes insurance without realising it. Chapter 6 provides guidance on how to avoid accidentally breaking the law. It looks at how insurance has been defined in case law and at how borderline cases have been decided, using key examples. There is also a section on when foreign insurers will be subject to the UK regulatory regime.

What is the law on one party acting as an agent or intermediary for another?

The distribution of insurance products often involves a middleman between the underwriter and policyholder. This makes agency law important in structuring agreements between insurers, intermediaries and corporate partners. Chapter 7 examines the (sometimes difficult) legal issues that arise from general law, over and above those arising from FSA regulation. The chapter also gives a preliminary guide to managing the risks of agency relationships.

How is the intermediary/corporate partner to be remunerated?

Chapter 8 discusses the issues arising from the different methods of paying intermediaries: commission; advances; profit sharing; and fees. The chapter also explains the normal methods of pricing insurance products and related regulatory issues.

What about client funds?

In the chain between policyholder and insurer, money is routinely channelled via the intermediary. The intermediary will hold insurers' and policyholders' funds when collecting premiums, handling refunds or when handling claims. Chapter 9 looks at the rules on holding client monies and, in particular, the difficult circumstances that arise if an intermediary becomes insolvent.

What about outsourcing?

Chapter 10 deals with the developments in outsourcing in general insurance and examines the regulatory and legal implications – including those under data protection law. The chapter deals with the practical considerations to be addressed by business executives and lawyers engaged in outsourcing arrangements. It includes checklists of clauses to be considered in such agreements.

What about information and communications technology?

Chapter 11 looks at the use of technology in insurance, concentrating on two areas: internet and e-commerce; and data handling. The chapter provides checklists for compliance with e-commerce laws and for data-sharing agreements.

Is competition law relevant?

Distribution arrangements between insurers and others must not give rise to anti-competitive behaviour. Chapter 12 examines the application of competition law to distribution arrangements with competitors and non-competitors as well as mergers and acquisitions. The chapter also includes a section on the recent European Union (EU) sector inquiry into business insurance and the UK market investigation of payment protection insurance.

Is employment law relevant?

The TUPE regulations can have a significant impact on both business transfer and service provision change transfer. The impact of this on insurance distribution arrangements is dealt with in Chapter 13 Part I.

Can insurance business be transferred without the specific consent of policyholders?

Yes, but only if the transfer procedure laid down in Part VII of FSMA is followed. The Part VII provisions are dealt with in Chapter 13 Part II. The specific rules for block transfer on renewal are dealt with in Chapter 13 Part III.

The regulatory framework for the insurance market

The sale and distribution of general insurance is now under the jurisdiction of the FSA. This chapter explains what this means.

I   The background

What's the relevant law?

The key statute governing general insurance is now the Financial Services and Markets Act 2000 (FSMA), which established the FSA. The principal provisions of the Act came into force at midnight on 30 November 2001, often known as N2. Under them, the FSA became the single 'super-regulator'.

FSMA replaced a two-tier structure. The FSA now discharges the functions not only of its predecessor the SIB (Securities and Investment Board) and the second-tier self-regulating organisations, but also the regulatory functions of other organisations in the financial services field.

As 'super-regulator', the FSA is intended to supervise *across* the financial services sector. One of the main effects of the Act is to bring together in one statute the regulation of those who provide financial services. Previously, they would have been regulated under the Insurance Companies Act 1982, the Financial Services Act 1986 and the Banking Act 1987 or under laws relating to building societies, friendly societies and credit unions.

When the decision was announced to create what has become the FSA, the Chancellor of the Exchequer Gordon Brown explained it like this: 'It is clear that the distinctions between different types of financial institution – banks, securities firms and insurance companies – are becoming increasingly blurred. Many of today's financial institutions are regulated by a plethora of different supervisors. This increases the cost and reduces the effectiveness of supervision.'

When were the FSA's powers extended?

FSMA removed most of the remaining elements of self-regulation. Two notable exceptions were for general insurance and mortgages. For the sale of general insurance there was the General Insurance Standards Council (GISC). For the sale of mortgages there was the Mortgage Code Compliance Board (MCCB).

However, both now fall within the remit of the FSA. On 31 October 2004, the provisions of FSMA, and consequently the full range of FSA powers, were extended to the sale of many mortgages. The sale of general insurance has been subject to FSA regulation since 14 January 2005 (although, as we shall see, some exemptions apply).

What are the FSA's objectives?

In carrying out its duties, the FSA has four statutory objectives. These are expressed in terms of market confidence, public awareness, consumer protection and combating financial crime. The FSA is also required to have regard to further considerations in discharging its duties; essentially, these amount to efficiency, management responsibility, proportionality, innovation and minimising the adverse effects of competition.

Where are the FSA Rules laid down?

Since N2, any person or entity wishing to carry on regulated general insurance business lawfully has had to be either FSA authorised or exempt. With authorisation comes the requirement to comply with the body of FSA regulation.

FSMA requires the FSA to set standards for the regulated firms (and also for itself) through rules, codes, guidance, directions and other arrangements. These are gathered together in the FSA Handbook, available online at www.fsa.gov.uk. The Handbook is structured and generally well written, but it is very, very long. What's more, it is a 'live' document, subject to frequent updates.

As well as containing rules (many of them derived from previous regulators), it contains general guidance, which comprises by far the greatest section of the Handbook in terms of size. ('General guidance' is to be distinguished from individual guidance, given by the FSA to a specific firm about its specific circumstances.)

In addition, there are 'Handbook guides' for small firms and for participants in the various financial services sectors. A testament to the size of the FSA Handbook is that the glossary itself runs to over 200 pages.

The FSA is trying to simplify the Handbook and, consequently, various changes are being made. They include an attempt to regulate more by way of principles; the intention is to remove some of the detailed rules. The FSA's own review of the Handbook concluded that the Conduct of Business rules for investment contracts (COB) had become 'increasingly difficult for users to navigate and understand – and therefore comply with'.

The FSA has made some moves towards separate tailored (or abridged) handbooks for different sectors. Also available on the FSA website, these include handbooks for 'life insurers with sales arms' and for 'intermediaries selling investments only'. There are different tailored handbooks for intermediaries selling combinations of investments, mortgages and general insurance, including one specifically for general insurance intermediaries.

Details of the sections of the Handbook relevant to general insurance are provided in Chapters 3 and 4.

II   The structure of FSA regulation

What's the source of FSA power?

There is a six-part structure to the FSA regulation of the sale of insurance:

1. A statutory prohibition on the carrying out of (widely defined) regulated activities without authorisation or exemption – Section 19 of FSMA. This is known as the general prohibition.
2. A statutory instrument: the Regulated Activities Order (RAO) or, to give it its full title, The Financial Services and Markets Act 2000 (Regulated Activities) Order 2001 SI2001/544. The RAO sets out

numerous exclusions – which, subject to conditions, narrow the scope of regulated activities.

3. Extensive (perimeter) guidance in PERG, a Regulatory Guide which sits alongside the Handbook.

4. Severe statutory sanctions for carrying out regulated activities without authorisation. Breach of the general prohibition is a criminal offence. The penalties can include imprisonment. (See the section 'What happens when FSMA or the Rules are broken?', below.)

5. Detailed FSA Rules for those authorised firms carrying out regulated activities. These include rules generally applicable to all authorised firms and also specific rules relating to conduct of business.

6. FSA investigation of and disciplinary action for authorised firms that breach FSA Rules in the carrying out of regulated activities. (See the section 'What happens when FSMA or the Rules are broken?', below.)

Running alongside the general prohibition concerning regulated activities is a parallel regime governing financial promotions, i.e. the promotion of financial products, including insurance. There is a financial promotion restriction in Section 21 of FSMA, and the consequences of breaching it are similar to those for contravention of the general prohibition.

Any individual or entity wishing to make or approve a financial promotion needs to be FSA authorised. (In practice, of course, a firm that is not authorised is unlikely to apply to the FSA solely to make financial promotions; a better route in such circumstances may be to arrange for the financial promotion to be approved by an authorised person, an option permissible under Section 21.)

What's the position of insurers?

Being an insurer – i.e. an underwriter of general insurance contracts and a 'principal' in the distribution chain – has long been a regulated activity. You cannot perform the functions of 'effecting contracts of insurance as principal' or 'carrying out contracts of insurance as principal' unless you're licensed to do so by the FSA. (There is an exclusion for vehicle breakdown insurance under Article 12 of the RAO – principally for the benefit of motoring organisations – but, generally, the exceptions are very limited.)

Each of the two functions – effecting and carrying out – is a regulated activity in its own right. In broad terms, 'effecting contracts of insurance' involves more than just making the contract. It includes the underwriting process, entry into the contract, preparations such as offering and negotiating insurance business, confirmation of cover and the actual issuing of the policy.

A practical application of this was in the *Re Great Western Assurance* case described in more detail on pages 65–66.

By contrast, 'carrying out contracts of insurance' refers to activities after the contract of insurance has been made but in connection with it – such as handling claims and the settlement and payment of claims.

The FSA regulation of an insurer is much more intense than the regime for insurance mediation. The main reason is that the consequences of insolvency of an insurer are potentially disastrous – and much more significant than insolvency of an intermediary. Accordingly, the capital and solvency requirements for insurers are stringent. Insurers must maintain adequate capital resources, which are monitored via reports to and dialogue with the FSA. Capital resources and solvency are also monitored at the group level.

The process for authorisation is also much tougher and, in practice, more expensive in terms of both resources and planning. Some intermediaries may, having obtained FSA authorisation for insurance mediation, consider that they could extract more of the value in their insurance operation by also becoming an authorised insurer. This is not a step to be taken lightly.

What insurance mediation activities are regulated by the FSA?

The regulated activities may be summarised as follows.

Dealing in contracts of insurance as agent (Article 21 RAO)

This activity is defined in terms of buying, selling, subscribing for or underwriting contracts as agent, whether for the insured or the insurer.

Where intermediaries commit an insurance undertaking to provide insurance for prospective policyholders – i.e. have delegated authority to bind an insurer to contracts – they're carrying out a regulated activity. This applies whether or not any advice is given and even if the intermediary deals through another authorised person – i.e. instructs another agent to enter into the contract on a client's behalf.

Intermediaries are also carrying out regulated business when they agree, on behalf of a prospective policyholder, to buy an insurance policy.

Arranging (bringing about) deals in contracts of insurance (Article 25(1) RAO)

A person brings about a contract of insurance if their involvement in the chain of events leading to the contract is *necessary* – i.e. there would be no policy without it.

Examples include:

- negotiating the terms of the contract on behalf of the customer with the insurance undertaking (and vice versa);
- assisting in the completion of a proposal form and sending it to the insurance undertaking; and
- entering into a contract of insurance as agent.

Making arrangements with a view to transactions in contracts of insurance (Article 25(2) RAO)

This activity is closely related to the arranging activity above. The difference is that it does not have to *bring about* the transaction to which it relates.

People perform this regulated activity when they, for example: help potential policyholders fill in or check application forms; introduce customers to an intermediary either for advice or to help arrange an insurance policy. In both cases, the participant is playing an *active* part in the distribution chain. The passive activity of merely displaying literature advertising insurance does not count under 25(2). There is a further exclusion for those who introduce insurance 'incidentally' – see page 53.

Assisting in the administration *and* performance of a contract of insurance (Article 39A RAO)

This relates to activities undertaken by intermediaries after the conclusion of a contract, for and on behalf of policyholders, in particular, claims management.

The application of Article 39A is not as wide as it first appears. FSA guidance is that merely *advising about* claims would not be enough to be caught. The intermediary must assist the policyholder not only in the administration of the policy but also in the performance of their contractual obligations. Further, claims management on behalf of most insurers is excluded by Article 39B. (For more details see Chapter 5.) The best example of a regulated activity under 39A is where an intermediary notifies a claim under a policy and then provides evidence in support of it or helps negotiate its settlement on the policyholder's behalf.

Advising on contracts of insurance (Article 53 RAO)

The advice must relate to a particular contract of insurance, be given to a person in their capacity as investor or potential investor and relate to the merits of a person buying, selling, subscribing for or underwriting a contract of insurance. Simply providing information is not a regulated activity.

According to the FSA, information is likely to be 'advice' if the circumstances give it the force of a recommendation. Typical recommendations and whether they will be regulated as advice are set out in PERG 5.8.5. The decisive factor is whether or not a *specific policy* is implied. 'I recommend you take the ABC insurer's motor insurance policy' would be regulated advice; 'I recommend that you take out motor insurance' would usually not.

Many insurers now use pre-purchase questioning and/or decision tree methods. There is detailed guidance at PERG 5.8 on the extent to which pre-purchase questioning or decision trees will constitute advice and what amounts to a regulated activity.

Agreeing to carry on a regulated activity (Article 64 RAO)

That is, agreeing to carry on any of the activities listed above.

What's the rule for renewals?

Invitations to renew policies, recommendations to renew existing cover and the subsequent effecting of the renewal are likely to be classed as regulated insurance mediation activities. This may be true even in the case of 'tacit renewals' – i.e. where a policyholder need take no action to maintain the cover.

When do exceptions apply?

The 'by way of business' test

For something to constitute a regulated activity it has to be carried on 'by way of business'.

The test of what is 'by way of business' is set out in FSMA (Carrying on Regulated Activities By Way of Business) Order 2001 SI 2001/1177. This provides, at article 3(4), that a person is not to be regarded as carrying on any insurance mediation activity unless they take up or pursue that activity for remuneration. FSA guidance indicates that 'remuneration' is to be broadly interpreted, and that it does not have to be provided or identified separately from remuneration for other goods or services.

An example of what the FSA would consider remuneration is where, instead of a fee or commission, a person receives a discount on their own premiums. Conversely, typical examples of where the business test is unlikely to be satisfied include:

■ arrangements made by a person for members of his or her family;
■ where employers provide insurance benefits for staff; and
■ where affinity groups or clubs set up insurance benefits for members.

In each case, there must be no direct financial benefit to the arranger. If, for example, an affinity group is receiving a commission or fee – or some other form of direct financial benefit – then the test is met and their activities are regulated.

'Connected contracts'

Some general insurance contracts are excluded from the ambit of 'insurance mediation' and therefore from the need for authorisation. The two principal exclusions are for travel insurance sold through a travel agent and extended warranties (e.g. on household electrical goods) sold by the vendor. The technical term for these exclusions is 'connected contracts'. The exclusions only apply if strict conditions are met – see Chapter 5 for more information.

Exclusion to Article 25(2) RAO

Article 72C RAO provides an important potential exclusion for people whose principal business is other than insurance mediation activities. This exclusion is explained more fully in Chapter 5.

Which Business Standards regime has to be followed?

The FSA's ICOB regime – laid down in the third block of the Handbook, Business Standards – applies to non-investment general insurance contracts such as household and car insurance and critical illness cover. The sale and distribution of insurance contracts with an investment element is governed by the older, generally more prescriptive, regime, COB. This means that life insurance, which often has an investment element, or can be used for investment, is typically regulated under COB. (In late 2007, the FSA will replace COB with a new version – referred to as 'NEWCOB' – which will adopt a more principles based approach.)

Inevitably, however, there are borderline cases – i.e. contracts that seem to fall between the two regimes. Some protection policies operate rather as a hybrid. Only certain 'pure' protection contracts come under ICOB; and pure protection policies are strictly defined by the FSA. Broadly, the term covers certain types of policy which pay out only on death or incapacity due to injury, sickness or infirmity.

Points to note are:

a) care has to be taken to recognise contracts with an investment element, which are subject to a stricter regime;
b) pure protection contracts may fall outside the investment regime subject to meeting the strict definition; but
c) the rules in ICOB do not always apply to pure protection contracts.

What happens when FSMA or the Rules are broken?

Breaches by unauthorised firms

The sanctions for breach of the general prohibition are very serious. There are four principal consequences:

■ criminal liability;
■ unenforceability of agreements;
■ liability for compensation; and
■ action by the FSA or the Department of Trade and Industry (DTI) to obtain an injunction and restitution.

Criminal liability

A breach of the general prohibition is punishable by up to two years' imprisonment and an unlimited fine.

It is a defence to establish that the accused took all reasonable precautions and exercised all due diligence to avoid committing the offence. The burden of proof is on the accused.

Importantly, the most severe sanction, imprisonment, is available not only when individuals act in their own capacity but when they act on behalf of (unauthorised) organisations. Further, mere negligence can give rise to criminal liability: there does not have to be an intention to break the law.

The relevant provisions are contained in Section 400 of FSMA. By Section 400(1), an officer of a body corporate is guilty of an offence committed by that body corporate if the offence was perpetrated with their consent or connivance, and attributable to any negligence on their part.

'Officer' is widely defined in Section 400(5) to include 'a director, member of the committee of management, chief executive, manager, secretary or other similar officer of the body'. Further, the same subsection extends the provisions to those who, while not formally appointed, purport to act in any such capacity. By Section 400(5)(b), the provisions also extend to individual controllers.

There are similar provisions for partners of firms and for officers of unincorporated associations and members of their governing bodies.

In summary, where an officer (as defined) of a company permits a regulated activity to be carried out or a financial promotion to be made by their (unauthorised) company through negligence or lack of knowledge, they run the risk of a two-year prison sentence.

If a company breaches the general prohibition or financial promotion restriction it will materially help its defence if it can show it sought proper professional advice as part of the process of 'taking all reasonable precautions and exercising all due diligence'.

Unenforceable agreements and compensation
The second and third consequences of breaching the general prohibition or financial promotion restriction are that:

∎ any resulting agreement is unenforceable against the customer;
∎ the customer is entitled to recover:
   a) any money or other property paid or transferred by them under the agreement; and
   b) compensation for any loss.

These are the provisions contained in Sections 26–30 of FSMA. However, the court does have discretion in applying them. The test is whether enforcing the agreement would be 'just and equitable'. If the court is satisfied that it is (given the circumstances of the case), it may allow the agreement to stand and the money/property that has been paid/transferred to be retained.

The following will be relevant factors in the 'test': whether the applicant (i.e. the person in breach of the general prohibition or financial promotion restriction) *reasonably believed* that they were not in breach; whether (in cases of breaches of the financial promotion restriction) the agreement was entered into as a *consequence* of the unlawful promotion.

These factors again highlight the importance of taking professional advice. If a company/individual accidentally breaches the general prohibition or financial promotion restriction it can avoid the worst consequences by proving that it took proper precautions. As well as being a defence against criminal prosecution, proof of such precautions may persuade the court that it is just and equitable for the agreement to be enforced.

Injunctions and restitution
The FSA and the DTI are entitled to seek injunctions to restrain future/anticipated contravention of the general prohibition or restriction on financial promotion. Similarly, application may be made by the FSA or DTI for orders to repay profits wrongly accrued or losses or adverse effects suffered. The court applications will be made under Section 380 (for injunctions) or Section 382 (for restitution orders) of FSMA.

Breaches by authorised firms

Breach by authorised firms of the Rules is not in itself a criminal offence. Nonetheless, the consequences can be serious.

The main one is FSA discipline. The FSA's principal disciplinary powers are:

- public statements and public censure under Section 205 of FSMA;
- financial penalties under Section 206;
- cancellation of permission for an authorised firm or withdrawal of approval from an individual.

The sanction chosen by the FSA will fit the nature and gravity of the offence.

A further consequence is exposure to claims for damages. By Section 150 of FSMA, a private person who suffers loss as a result of a contravention of an FSA rule has the right to sue for breach of statutory duty (subject to some limited exceptions). This right to damages is in addition to any other right in contract law or tort.

When is an authorised firm criminally liable under FSMA?

Section 397 makes it a criminal offence to make misleading statements. The offence is committed if both: 1) a person makes a materially false or misleading or deceptive statement either knowingly or recklessly, or dishonestly conceals a material fact; and 2) the act or omission is for the purpose of inducing another person to enter into a relevant agreement (broadly, an agreement under FSMA).

Appointed representative regulations

As we have seen, authorisation by the FSA protects firms and their 'officers' from criminal prosecution, but brings with it a considerable compliance burden. Because of this, many intermediaries and distributors seek appointed representative status. Appointed representatives (ARs) act for an authorised principal (often, but not always, an insurer) and thereby effectively transfer regulatory responsibility. They are exempt from authorisation.

The regime covering appointed representatives is explained in more detail in Chapter 5 (see pages 56–57), but key points to bear in mind include:

- there must be a written agreement under which the principal agrees to accept regulatory responsibility but stipulates that the AR follows the Rules (it clearly cannot discharge its responsibilities unless the AR toes the line);

- the AR is only exempt from the general prohibition if it sticks to those activities for which the principal takes responsibility;
- ARs are recorded on the FSA Register available for public inspection; and
- they can only carry out activities as listed on the Register.

Where an appointed representative is contractually permitted to act for more than one principal, those principals are required to enter into a multiple principal agreement. The main purpose, from the regulatory point of view, is to ensure a clear apportionment of responsibility for dealing with complaints and issues in relation to the AR. However, a multiple principal agreement has its complications, and advice should be sought.

Appointed representatives come in two forms: 'full' AR and 'introducer' AR. The latter are limited to introducing activities and are subject to a slightly lighter regime.

3

Obligations of a regulated firm

The Financial Services and Markets Act 2000 required the FSA to exercise its rule-making power through 'a rule-making instrument'. That instrument is the FSA Handbook.

An exhaustive document, running to several thousand pages, the Handbook contains the obligations of all regulated firms – i.e. both general and sector-specific rules and provisions. It consists of seven main blocks, each subdivided into modules (sourcebooks or manuals) known by abbreviated reference codes – for example, PRIN for Principles for Businesses.

In its Reader's Guide to the Handbook, the FSA says it expects most firms to refer regularly only to those parts directly relevant to their businesses. The purpose of this and the following chapter is to introduce some of the main areas that concern those involved in the sale and distribution of insurance.

This chapter sets out some of the more important general high-level rules and guidance. The detailed rules for the conduct of insurance business are the subject of Chapter 4.

What's behind the rules?

In making and enforcing rules and guidance the FSA takes into account the four objectives given to it by Parliament in Section 2(2) of FSMA:

■ market confidence;
■ public awareness of the financial system;
■ the protection of consumers; and
■ the reduction of financial crime.

The protection of consumers objective is defined in Section 5(1) of FSMA as 'securing the *appropriate degree* of protection for consumers'. This is developed further in Section 5(2):

> In considering what degree of protection may be appropriate, the Authority must have regard to:
>
> a) the differing degrees of risk involved in different kinds of investment or other transaction;
> b) the differing degrees of experience and expertise that different consumers may have in relation to different kinds of regulated activity;
> c) the needs that consumers may have for advice and accurate information; and
> d) the general principle that consumers should take responsibility for their decisions.

What are the FSA Principles?

The FSA Principles for Businesses are set out in Block 1 of the Handbook, High Level Standards – those 'standards that apply to *all* firms and approved persons' (our italics). They're informed by the statutory objectives listed above. The Principles are set out as follows:

1. A firm must conduct its business with integrity.
2. A firm must conduct its business with due skill, care and diligence.
3. A firm must take reasonable care to organise and control its affairs responsibly and effectively, with adequate risk management systems.
4. A firm must maintain adequate financial resources.
5. A firm must observe proper standards of market conduct.
6. A firm must pay due regard to the interests of its customers and treat them fairly.
7. A firm must pay due regard to the information needs of its clients, and communicate information to them in a way that is clear, fair and not misleading.
8. A firm must manage conflicts of interest fairly, both between itself and its customers and between a customer and another client.

9. A firm must take reasonable care to ensure the suitability of its advice and discretionary decisions for any customer who is entitled to rely upon its judgement.
10. A firm must arrange adequate protection for clients' assets when it is responsible for them.
11. A firm must deal with its regulators in an open and co-operative way, and must disclose to the FSA appropriately anything relating to the firm of which the FSA would reasonably expect notice.

The Principles are very important. Breaching them could lead to a fine, public censure, or, in the most serious cases, cancellation of the firm's authorisation (thereby rendering it unable to continue the regulated activity).

What's the relationship between the Principles and FSA Rules?

The detailed Rules, set out in the modules of the Handbook, emanate from and are an elaboration of the Principles: the Principles underpin the entire Handbook. There is often an obvious and direct relationship between the Principles and Rules. For example, Principle 10 requiring 'adequate protection for clients' assets' is specifically extended by the detailed Client Assets Sourcebook (CASS) rules relating to client money (discussed in Chapter 9).

A breach of the Rules is likely to be a breach of the Principles and (often) vice versa. Indeed, in disciplinary action against firms, the FSA will often cite a breach of the Principles as well as a breach of the specific Rules.

Where firms have been disciplined for breach of the financial promotion (i.e. advertising) rules they have also been disciplined for breaches of Principles 2, 3, 7 and 8. Breaches of Principles 3 and 7 appear in virtually every financial promotion case (see Chapter 4, section III).

But the Principles also stand on their own. Breach of the Principles is in itself sufficient grounds for disciplinary action. In 2005, a very significant fine was imposed for breach of the Principles without a concurrent breach of the Rules.

The Principles tend to fill any gaps in the detailed Rules. This means it is generally a fruitless exercise to seek to avoid the spirit of the Rules by looking for 'loopholes'. A good working guideline is 'if it is in breach of the spirit of the Rules, then it is in breach of the Principles'.

What are the practical implications of Principle 11?

Principle 11 is particularly important. It requires notice to the FSA of *anything* of which the FSA would *reasonably expect* notice. There is a (non-exhaustive) list of examples in the supervision manual (SUP) of Block 4 (SUP 15.3.8). It includes:

- setting up a new undertaking;
- commencing the provision of cross-border services;
- commencing the provision of a new type of product or service;
- ceasing or significantly reducing a regulated activity;
- entering into a material outsourcing arrangement (see Chapter 10, pages 104–15);
- any significant failure in the firm's systems or controls;
- action that would result in a material change in capital adequacy or solvency.

Principle 11 also in effect requires an authorised firm to police itself and, where necessary, to report itself for serious breaches. SUP 15.3.11 states that:

> 1) A firm must notify the FSA of a significant breach of a Rule or Principle ...
> 2) A firm must make the notification immediately it becomes aware ...

Breach of (or compliance with) Principle 11 can make a significant difference to the extent of any penalty imposed by the FSA.

A natural response for firms when considering the application of Principle 11 is to be cautious and 'if in doubt, disclose'. The logic is that if the issue turns out to be of little or no interest to the FSA, then minimal damage will have been done. Conversely, if firms are embarrassed or fearful about the consequences of disclosure to the FSA, that in itself would seem enough reason to come clean.

What are the conditions for FSA authorisation?

Block 1 of the Handbook also sets out the threshold conditions. These are the minimum statutory conditions needed to obtain and retain FSA authorisation. Essentially, a firm will not be able to carry on regulated activities as an insurance intermediary unless:

1. its close links (e.g. any parent or subsidiary or fellow group member) do not prevent or hinder FSA supervision;
2. it has adequate financial and non-financial resources and adequate means of managing them; and
3. it is suitable, e.g. has 'fit and proper' personnel.

(Relevant matters include integrity, competent and prudent management and the exercise of due skill, care and diligence; see 'Approved Persons', below.)

There are additional threshold conditions for insurers. The firm will not be able to carry on the regulated activities of effecting or carrying out insurance contracts in the UK unless it complies with the threshold conditions 1–3 above, and it:

4. is a body corporate (other than a limited liability partnership), a registered friendly society or a member of Lloyd's; and
5. is located in and does business in the UK (e.g. has a head office or registered office here) and, in the case of motor vehicle liability insurance, has a claims representative in every other state of the European Economic Area (EEA).

Conditions 1 and 2 need further explanation. The main purpose of the close links rule (threshold condition 1) is to give the FSA an overview of ownership and control of the applicant and of those organisations that it owns or controls. Close links diagrams can be very complex; a 20 per cent involvement is sufficient to render an organisation a parent or subsidiary. Close links to a company subject to the laws and regulations of a state outside the EEA may prevent effective supervision by the FSA.

Authorised firms have ongoing obligations in relation to notification to the FSA of changes in close links.

The second threshold condition requires, in effect, the FSA to form a view of the resources available to the firm and to have regard to the impact (positive or negative) of its position within a group. A firm's resources must be sufficient for the activities it undertakes. The FSA may take into account the fact the authorised entity is a member of a group.

What does the Handbook say about governance?

Internal systems and controls

The SYSC module, Senior Management Arrangements, Systems and Controls, covers some of the key governance issues for regulated firms.

One or more individuals must be allocated to apportion responsibilities among directors and senior managers and to oversee the establishment and maintenance of systems and controls. The apportionment and allocation of responsibilities must be clear and appropriate and it must be recorded. The practical consequence is that organisational charts and diagrams, together with job descriptions, should be maintained. Job descriptions must fit into the structure and reflect reality.

The nature and extent of the systems and controls should be proportionate to the firms and, in particular, the size, complexity and degree of risk involved in their business. Many firms have a compliance function; but a compliance function is not mandatory. Whether a compliance function is needed is discussed in SYSC 3.2.7.

As well as discussing the need (or otherwise) for a compliance function, SYSC 3.2 sets out guidance on anti-money-laundering systems and controls, risk assessment, management information, the use of employees and agents, audit committees and internal audits, business strategy, remuneration policies, business continuity and the making and keeping of records. SYSC 3.2, therefore, constitutes a checklist of risk issues.

Similarly, SYSC 13 'Operational Risk: Systems and Controls' has a useful list of items for consideration. SYSC 13.9, for example, sets out what a firm should do before entering into an outsourcing arrangement (SYSC 13A.9.4) and also relevant terms to include in a contract with a service provider (SYSC 13A.9.5). For executives and lawyers dealing with outsourcing contracts these provisions are an excellent starting point. (The management of the risks in outsourcing is discussed in Chapter 10.)

Approved Persons

Individuals carrying out 'controlled functions' are subject to the 'Approved Persons' regime (APER and FIT). A firm must obtain prior approval of an individual from the FSA before that person can carry out a controlled function.

The regime applies both to the direct employees of an authorised firm and to other persons acting under an arrangement between the firm and a 'contractor', such as an appointed representative (see Chapter 5, pages 56 and 57). The source of the FSA's powers in relation to Approved Persons is section 59 of FSMA.

Controlled functions

There are many controlled functions (CFs). They are divided into two main types: type 1, for those who have 'significant influence' on their firm's conduct; and type 2, for those who deal with customers. However, the customer functions apply to investment business not general insurance.

The significant influence functions are subdivided into governing functions, required functions, systems and control functions and significant management functions. (Despite the terminology, not all authorised firms *require* individuals for all controlled functions.) Details of the controlled functions are at SUP 10.4.5.

Standards of conduct

Approved Persons are subject to the terms of the Statement of Principles and Code of Practice for Approved Persons contained in APER. Principles 1 to 4 apply to all Approved Persons and Principles 5 to 7 to those performing a significant influence function. Principles 1 to 3 require an Approved Person to act with integrity, due skill, care and diligence and to observe proper standards of market conduct. Principle 4 requires the Approved Person to deal with the FSA in an open and co-operative way and to disclose appropriately any information of which the FSA would reasonably expect notice. In other words, an Approved Person who becomes aware of significant breaches of a Rule or Principle should ensure that the firm notifies the FSA.

The fitness test

An Approved Person is one fit and proper to perform the controlled function. The rules are contained in FIT 1.3.1. The 'fitness test' will centre on:

a) honesty, integrity and reputation;
b) competence and capability; and
c) financial soundness.

The effect of the regime

The Approved Persons regime means that the system for the authorisation/registration of firms is extended to individuals. It exposes the Approved Person personally to the rigours of FSA discipline, including fines, censure and the withdrawal of approval to act in a controlled function. The practical effect, particularly for senior managers/directors, can be, in extreme circumstances, to terminate the ability to act in a senior capacity in the financial services industry.

The seriousness of the Approved Person's liability is demonstrated in a recent case against the chief executive of an insurance broker. The chief executive was responsible for ensuring that the broker complied with the FSA's client money rules at CASS. The auditors identified serious failings in the client money systems; the director had neither known nor enquired whether the company was complying with those rules. As an Approved Person, he was held to have personal responsibility. He was fined £17,500 in September 2006.

What are the general rules for employees?

The Training and Competence Rules (contained in the T&C module of the third block of the Handbook, Business Standards) apply generally and require all firms to ensure that employees are competent for the activities they carry out. Training failures have been cited when organisations have been disciplined – for example, for breaches of the financial promotion rules, discussed in more detail in the third section of the next chapter.

The relevant T&C rules include:

2.3.1 If a firm's employees engage in or oversee an activity with or for private customers, the firm must:
  (1) At intervals appropriate to the circumstances, determine the training needs of those employees and organise appropriate training to address these needs; and
  (2) ensure that training is timely, planned, appropriately structured and evaluated.
2.6 A firm must have appropriate arrangements in place to ensure that an employee who has been assessed as competent to engage in or oversee an activity maintains competence.

Notices in relation to Approved Persons

The application for FSA approval under Section 59 of FSMA must be made by completing Form A (included as part of the application pack for FSA permission to carry on regulated activities). It must cover employment history over the past five years and give the reasons for leaving previous employment.

When a person ceases to perform a controlled function, the FSA must be notified on another form, Form C.

Importantly, the FSA must be given immediate notice if the firm has information that reasonably suggests that it will submit a *qualified* Form C. Form C is qualified if the Approved Person has been dismissed, has resigned while under investigation or if there is a question mark over their fitness and propriety.

Form E is to be used if a firm wishes to transfer an Approved Person to another (internal) controlled function.

The rules and guidance for these notices are to be found at 10.11 to 10.13 of SUP in the Regulatory Processes block.

Other FSA Handbook rules and guidance

This chapter has focused mainly on the High Level Standards block. A brief description of some of the other parts of the Handbook is given below:

- **Prudential Standards (Block 2).**This contains the prudential requirements for insurers and insurance intermediaries, as well as other regulated firms. The rules include the FSA's requirements as to capital adequacy; naturally, the rules are very demanding for insurers.
- **Business Standards (Block 3).**These contain the conduct of business rules for investments (COB), for general insurance (ICOB) and for mortgages (MCOB). The Business Standards sections also include the client assets rules (CASS) discussed in Chapter 9 and the training and competence rules referred to above.
- **Regulatory Processes (Block 4).**This contains the manuals on authorisation, supervision, enforcement and decision making. The authorisation manual provides guidance on the circumstances in which registration is needed, the procedures for applying for it and the FSA's powers in relation to it.
- **Specialist Sourcebooks (Block 6).**There is a series of specialist sourcebooks relating to particular situations, including one set of rules relating specifically to Lloyd's.
- **Handbook Guides.** As well as rules for some special areas, there are useful Handbook Guides for small mortgage and insurance intermediaries. The purpose is to provide an easier and more accessible set of rules for such firms/people.
- **Regulatory Guides.** This includes the Perimeter Guidance Manual, which provides further guidance on whether authorisation is needed and on exclusions under FSMA.

4

The Insurance Conduct of Business Rules

The Insurance Conduct of Business Rules (ICOB Rules) form a separate module in the FSA Handbook. They relate to non-investment insurance contracts, i.e. general insurance contracts such as household and motor insurance and certain pure protection contracts such as permanent health policies. They do not apply to products such as long-term care cover or endowments and life policies with an investment element. These are covered by their 'older relative' – the FSA's Conduct of Business Rules (COB), aimed specifically at firms with investment business customers. (See the box on page 46.)

In March 2007, the FSA announced that it would be revising ICOB to adopt a more principles-based approach. The proposals are to remove most of the specific requirements which go beyond the minimum standards required by the EU Insurance Mediation Directive, but introduce some specific protections for personal protection products such as payment protection insurance and critical illness cover, which it sees as high risk. These changes are likely to take place in December 2007. This chapter reflects the law at the time this book went to press.

The ICOB Rules consist of eight main chapters relating to the sale and administration of non-investment insurance. In this chapter, we look at the key points and principles of each one.

I Application and purpose (ICOB 1)

Whom do the Rules protect?

Put simply, the customer (that is, policyholders or prospective policy-holders) – especially if they are a retail customer, i.e. acting outside their trade, business or profession.

Fewer ICOB rules relate to commercial customers.

Who must comply?

Firms

The ICOB rules apply to insurers and insurance intermediaries. ICOB applies to insurers in their role as product providers and when they are undertaking insurance mediation activities (for example, when an insurer arranges or advises on insurance contracts through its sales force). Where a chain of intermediaries exists between the insurer and the customer, ICOB applies only to the intermediary in contact with the customer, not the intermediaries in the middle of the chain (although such intermediaries will, of course, still need to be authorised to carry on regulated activities). ICOB also applies to managing agents at Lloyd's and motor vehicle liability insurers.

A table summarising who is affected under each chapter of the ICOB Rules is given in Annex 1 to ICOB 1.

Appointed representatives

When an insurer or an insurer's intermediary appoints someone as their appointed representative ('AR') (see Chapter 5, pages 56 and 57), they retain ultimate responsibility for the acts of the AR. It is important, therefore, that any contract with an AR details ICOB compliance requirements. There must be a system whereby the principal (e.g. the insurer) can fulfil all its legal and obligatory duties – be it directly or indirectly through the AR. (See section IV for more on ARs.)

Third-party processors

It is not uncommon, as Chapter 10 makes clear, for those in the insurance business to outsource regulated activities such as policy administration. Special rules apply to the outsource providers when they are 'third-party processors' as defined in the FSA Handbook. (See section IV, below.)

Are there any exceptions?

ICOB does not apply to activities relating to reinsurance contracts or to certain large risks for commercial customers located *outside* the European Economic Area (EEA).

The rules are also of limited or varying application for:

- service companies;
- authorised professional firms;
- group policies; and
- insurance mediation activities undertaken for commercial customers in respect of 'large risks' located *within* the EEA. (Large risks include: aircraft, ships and railway rolling stock; certain credit and suretyship contracts; and property and liability contracts.)

II General rules (ICOB 2)

What are the main rules?

There are several general rules/principles in ICOB. Three of the most important – and potentially most troublesome for firms – are considered below.

Communications must be clear, fair and not misleading (ICOB 2.2.3R)

This rule applies to all communications with customers – written and spoken or electronic. It restates, as a separate rule, part of Principle 7 of the Principles for Businesses in the FSA Handbook. By doing so, it gives a private person the right to bring an action for damages if they suffer any loss as a result of a firm communicating information in a way that is unclear, unfair or misleading. (Contravention of the Principles in PRIN does not do this.)

Unfair inducements (ICOB 2.3.2R)

The unfair inducements rule in ICOB 2 prohibits a firm (and any person acting for it) offering or accepting inducements if they are likely to conflict to a material extent with any duty that the firm or the recipient firm owes to customers. The rule covers financial and non-financial inducements – including cash or a cash equivalent, commission, hospitality and training programmes (ICOB 2.3.4G).

ICOB does not impose an outright ban on specific inducement such as volume overrides or profit-share arrangements or prevent a firm from giving indirect benefits (see Chapter 8 on pricing and remuneration). Whether the inducement gives rise to a conflict will depend not only on the inducement itself but on the surrounding circumstances and whether the inducement was operated fairly.

As well as the unfair inducement rule in ICOB 2.3.2, a firm must consider the FSA Principles, in particular Principle 6 (acting with due regard to a customer's interests and treating them fairly) and the ability of the firm to comply with other rules in ICOB such as the suitability requirements (see section IV, below).

Inducements can give rise to conflicts and a firm must, in accordance with Principle 8, manage conflicts of interest – be they between itself and its customers or a customer and another client – fairly. The following are examples of situations where inducements could create material conflicts in contravention of ICOB 2.3 (and breach Principle 6 – treating customers fairly):

i) where an intermediary holds themselves out as getting the best deal for the customer and the inducement influences the intermediary's placement of business in a way that is contrary to the customer's interests – i.e. encourages the intermediary to mis-sell;

ii) where an intermediary is involved in the settling of claims but has a financial incentive which influences how he or she settles a customer's claim which is against the customer's interests.

Clearly, intermediaries selling to customers need to manage and control the risks inherent in certain remuneration structures for sales staff and intermediaries. However, the insurer must also ensure it does not structure inducements in a way that breaches the inducements rule (and/or the principle of treating customers fairly). Both the intermediary and the insurer must ensure they have adequate systems and controls to manage inducements and identify and remedy unfair inducements.

Excessive charges

It is worth noting that a separate rule has been introduced (ICOB 2.10.1R) which prohibits excessive charges for retail customers. ICOB provides guidance on matters firms should consider in determining whether a charge is excessive, which include considering whether the charge is an abuse of the trust of the retail customer. The rule on excessive charges does not apply to premiums but does cover fees (including fees charged by the intermediary where it doesn't receive commission from the insurer).

III   Financial promotion (ICOB 3)

Financial promotion has been a hot FSA topic over recent years. The FSA has set up a consumer hotline and a specific department to tackle the subject, published two key discussion documents in successive years about it – as well as quarterly bulletins and dedicated pages on its website – and issued general and specific financial promotion warnings.

And the FSA has meant business: there have been a number of high-profile fines for breach of the rules – including one for £500,000.

What is financial promotion?

'Financial promotion' is the 'communication of an invitation or inducement to engage in investment activity'. Financial promotions are only permitted if they are made or approved by an authorised person (generally, a body regulated by the FSA).

It can be seen that 'financial promotion' is very widely defined. As well as all conventional advertising media – television, radio, newspapers, posters – it covers messages in brochures, leaflets, even business cards.

Overall, however, the ICOB 3 financial promotion rules are comparatively 'light-touch' compared with their equivalent in COB 3. Their scope is significantly cut back by a number of exemptions (see below).

If a financial promotion is made (or approved) for a non-investment insurance contract then the rules in ICOB 3 have to be followed. ICOB 3 runs alongside and parallel to other ICOB chapters, particularly chapter 4, Advising and Selling Standards. Accordingly, it is possible that ICOB 3 and ICOB 4 will have to be considered simultaneously during the sales process. The fact that there is an exemption from the ICOB 3 rules does *not* mean that there is a similar exemption from ICOB 4.

What's the main rule?

The overriding principle is that promotions, like all forms of communication with customers (or potential customers), should be clear, fair and not misleading (ICOB 3.8).

This has some obvious implications. Among other things, it means that:

■ any comparisons or contrasts used for promotional purposes must be fair – i.e. with truly similar contracts;
■ the promotion must not create confusion in the marketplace – for example, between a firm and one of its competitors;

- small print cannot be used to qualify prominent claims;
- the accuracy of all material facts must be capable of being substantiated;
- phrases such as 'cheapest deal' must be qualified by a prominent statement of how the saving is to be achieved and any 'terms and conditions' – e.g. criteria the customer may have to meet;
- it should be clear whether quotations are actual or estimates;
- estimates should be representative of the premium that would be paid by someone in a similar position to the retail customer;
- statements of opinion should be honestly held and, if possible, given with the consent of the person concerned; and
- the FSA key facts logo, reproduced on customer information documents, should only be used if required by an FSA rule.

It is easy to see the kind of thing that would breach the ICOB 3.8 rule. The FSA has, for example, expressed concern about a financial promotion for general insurance that targeted customers in the London area but quoted a premium likely to be charged to a customer in the North West.

Are there any other rules?

There are two other important elements to ICOB 3:

1. A firm must be able to show that it has taken reasonable steps to ensure that promotions are clear, fair and not misleading. (In other words, the burden of proof is on the firm: records and systems and processes will form a big part of the 'defence' in any FSA investigation.)
2. Firms must (under ICOB 3.7) confirm their promotions are compliant. The confirmation must be by an individual with 'appropriate expertise'. A third party may undertake the 'confirmation exercise' but the responsibility remains with the firm. Again, records need to be kept in order to satisfy the FSA that there were 'reasonable steps'.

Other parts of the FSA Handbook also have to be borne in mind. All organisations that have been fined for breach of the financial promotion rules have also been found to have breached one of the Principles for Businesses and, in some cases, the rules on systems and controls in SYSC, the supervision rules in SUP or the training and competence rules in T&C.

What are the exemptions?

As stated earlier, some types of financial promotions are exempt. These include:

a) Promotions to commercial customers. For this exemption to apply, there must be:
  – a statement that the financial promotion is intended for commercial customers;
  – a statement that others should not rely on the promotion; and
  – a system in place to ensure that only commercial customers enter into contracts.
b) Generic promotions that do not identify an insurer. An insurance inter-mediary advertising their insurance mediation services ('I am an excellent broker and can give you a good service') would be exempt – provided their advertisement did not name an insurer.
c) Factual contact details: promotions that show only the name of the firm, the name of the contact, a logo, contact details and a brief description of the firm's products and fees. (This exemption can be used for business cards.)
d) Real-time communications – i.e. promotions made during the course of a personal visit, telephone conversation or other interactive dialogue.
e) One-off promotions that are communicated to and tailored exclusively for one recipient and do not form part of an organised marketing campaign.
f) Reinsurance contracts and contracts for large risks (which are excluded from ICOB generally as stated in section I above).
g) Communications from outside the UK, subject to the detailed provisions of Articles 30–33 of the Financial Promotion Order.

IV   Advising and selling standards (ICOB 4)

ICOB 4 is designed to ensure that customers are adequately informed about the service being provided by the insurance intermediary or insurer.

Insurance intermediaries who are in contact with the customer must disclose certain information about themselves. Insurers who are undertaking insurance mediation activities themselves (for example, because they are selling direct) have more limited disclosure requirements (ICOB 4.1.4R). However, both insurers and insurance intermediaries must ensure their appointed representatives comply with the requirements of ICOB 4. (An appointed representative must comply fully with the relevant status disclosure requirements in ICOB 4, even where its principal benefits from an exemption.)

The extent of the information to be provided to customers depends on whether the customer is a retail customer or a commercial customer.

What information must be provided?

'Status disclosure' for retail and commercial customers

The insurance intermediary (and, where appropriate the appointed representative) must provide certain information about itself to all customers in a durable medium unless certain exemptions apply. This information, known as 'status disclosure', is generally required by ICOB *before* conclusion of the contract and includes:

1. The intermediary's name and address.
2. The intermediary's statutory status – 'x is authorised and regulated by the Financial Services Authority' or 'y is an appointed representative of x, authorised and regulated by the Financial Services Authority'. (Annex 1 to part 4 of GEN, the General Provisions of the FSA Handbook, provides a guide to statutory status.)
3. That the information in (1) and (2) can be checked on the FSA's Register on the FSA's website or by contacting the FSA.
4. Details of any holdings the intermediary has in an insurance company, or that an insurance company (or its parent) has in the intermediary.
5. Whether the intermediary provides advice or information:
   (a) on the basis of a fair analysis of the market;
   (b) from a limited number of insurers; or
   (c) from a single insurer.
6. If the contract provided was not selected after a 'fair analysis' of the market, that the customer can request a copy of the list of the insurers the intermediary selects from or deals with. (Guidance on what constitutes 'fair analysis' is given at ICOB 4.2.11.)
7. The complaints procedure – that complaints may be referred to the Financial Ombudsman Service (FOS).
8. Compensation arrangements should the intermediary fail to meet its liabilities (i.e. whether the customer is covered by the Financial Services Compensation Scheme (FSCS)).

The ICOB rules do not specify the format in which the information summarised above must be provided to the customer, but there is an option to use an FSA 'template' – the 'initial disclosure document' or 'IDD'.

There are exemptions from the requirement to provide the information above in a *durable medium* before conclusion of the contract:

1) if the customer
   a) requests this; or
   b) requires immediate cover
      the information may be provided orally before the contract is concluded; or
2) in the case of telephone sales (subject to certain requirements being fulfilled).

In any of these cases the customer must be given the information above in a durable medium immediately after conclusion of the contract.

Disclosure requirements for introducers

If the intermediary merely introduces the customer to the insurer it need only provide certain (less detailed) information about itself 'in good time' before making the introduction: the name and address of the introducer, its statutory status under GEN 4 Annex I, details of any fees and whether the introducer is a member of the same group as the insurer it is introducing.

Disclosure requirements for third-party processors

A firm that is a Third Party Processor (as defined in the FSA Handbook) for another authorised firm ('A') may, for the purposes of the disclosure requirements, tell customers that it is the authorised firm ('A') rather than reveal its own identity.

For example, an insurer may outsource its telephone sales to a specialist call centre operator. The Third Party Processor rules would allow the call centre operator's staff to deal with customers in the name of the insurer, rather than having to explain that it is a different company.

To become a Third Party Processor, there must be an outsourcing contract which must (among other things) acknowledge that 'A' accepts responsibility for the activities carried on by the Third Party Processor on its behalf. Any authorised firm carrying on insurance mediation activities (or an AR acting for its principal – see Chapter 5) in relation to non-investment insurance contracts for another authorised firm (or an appointed representative) can be a Third Party Processor if it satisfies the definition in the FSA Handbook.

Information on fees

Retail and commercial customers must be given details of any fees before the customer is liable to pay them, or before conclusion of the contract, whichever is earlier. (Fees do not include premiums or commission that forms part of premium.)

Disclosure of commission

Details of commission received by the intermediary and any associate must be disclosed to a commercial customer – on request.

There are no FSA rules requiring disclosure of commission to retail customers, but general principles of agency law will still apply. Accordingly, customers have the right to demand that any intermediary acting on their behalf (rather than as agent for the insurer) discloses details of their remuneration. (See Chapter 7 which covers the principles of agency law in detail.)

What are the requirements for advised sales?

Suitability requirements (ICOB 4.3)

ICOB 4.3 applies when an intermediary advises a customer to buy a specific non-investment insurance contract (i.e. makes what the FSA Handbook calls a 'personal recommendation').

Any personal recommendation must be suitable for the customer's demands and needs. The rules set out what information the intermediary should obtain from customers to assess their demands and needs and what factors should be considered in the assessment.

Statement of demands and needs (ICOB 4.4)

Intermediaries must issue a 'demands and needs' statement to all customers (retail and commercial) on the sale and renewal of a non-investment insurance policy. (There are certain exemptions from this requirement for insurers in relation to commercial customers and non-advised sales to retail customers.)

The statement should do three basic things:

a) set out the customer's demands and needs;
b) confirm whether a personal recommendation has been made; and
c) where a personal recommendation has been made, explain the reasons for recommending that particular contract.

The content of the statement should reflect the complexity of the contract. ICOB 4.4.3G to ICOB 4.4.6G provide guidance on the style and presentation of the statement. If the contract is straightforward and no personal recommendation has been made, a generic statement can be made in the product information. An example may be: 'This product meets the demands and needs of those who wish to ensure that the veterinary needs of their pet are met now and in the future.'

V   Product disclosure (ICOB 5)

The FSA requires that certain information and certain documents relating to the insurance product are provided to the customer at various stages of the sales process.

What are the rules for retail customers?

The intermediary (or insurer when selling directly) must provide the retail customer with certain information about the insurance policy 'in good time' before conclusion of the contract.

A distance contract is one secured by telephone or other remote means. In the case of a non-distance contract, the customer should be informed, before conclusion of the contract, of the importance of reading the policy summary and be provided with, in a durable medium:

A.
- a policy summary outlining significant features of the policy, charges, exclusions and limitations and the complaints procedure – including how to refer a complaint to the FOS;
- a statement detailing the total price to be paid, whether and when it will be reviewed and charges or fees payable in addition to the premium;
- certain EU directive required information as set out in ICOB 5.5.20R (the directive requirements vary according to whether the contract is a pure protection contract or other non-investment contract and whether it is a 'distance contract').

Immediately after conclusion of the non-distance contract the retail customer must also be provided with the following in a durable medium:

B.
- the policy document (detailing all the terms of the insurance);
- information about the claims handling process;
- information on cancellation rights during the 'cooling off period' (see section VI below);
- information on applicable compensation cover (e.g. the retail customer may have recourse to the Financial Services Compensation Scheme.)

Where the sale is a distance contract, the information in A and B above must be provided to a retail customer 'in good time' before conclusion of the contract in

a durable medium unless one of the exemptions applies (e.g. in the case of telephone sales or where the customer gives his or her consent to receiving limited
information). In such cases (subject to certain requirements and the provision
of certain information beforehand) the insurer/intermediary may provide all
the information in A and B above 'immediately after conclusion of the
contract' in a durable medium.

What are the rules for commercial customers?

The ICOB product disclosure requirements are less onerous for commercial
customers:

1) Before conclusion of the contract, the customer must be given:
   - sufficient information to enable the commercial customer to make
     an informed decision;
   - the amount of premium and any fees; and
   - certain EU directive required information (as set out in ICOB
     5.5.20R) such as arrangements for complaints and, where appro-
     priate, the existence of an ombudsman, and information on the appli-
     cable law of the contract.
2) After conclusion of the contract, the policy document must be provided
   promptly. Where the policy is concluded over the telephone, the
   directive required information does not need to be given until immediately after conclusion of the contract.

VI   Cancellation (ICOB 6)

ICOB 6 provides that an insurer must offer retail customers a 'cooling-off
period' after entering into a contract and after each renewal. During the
cooling-off period the retail customer may cancel the contract (without
giving any reason) by serving notice on the insurer or its representative.

What are the cancellation periods?

1) 30 days for pure protection contracts;
2) 14 days for general insurance contracts; and
3) 30 days for mixed contracts – i.e. those that contain elements of both.

Where the insurer gives a retail customer a period exceeding the 14 or 30
days under the insurance contract, it must still disclose the right to cancel

under ICOB (6.2.1R) and make clear the distinction between the ICOB rule and the terms of the contract, which operate independently.

When does the cancellation period start?

The cooling off period will begin on the *later* of:

1) for a pure protection policy, the day the retail customer is informed the contract has been concluded; for a general insurance policy, the day of the conclusion of the contract; and
2) the day the retail customer receives the contractual terms and conditions and the information required under ICOB 5 in a durable medium.

In accordance with generally accepted principles of law, the insurer is entitled to assume that:

■ documents sent to the correct address by first class post on business day 1 are received on business day 2;
■ a fax is received when sent, if an appropriate transmission report is generated by the sender's machine; and
■ an e-mail is received when sent.

A retail customer may contradict these assumptions by supplying some kind of evidence – if he or she does so, the FSA Guidance states that the insurer should generally accept such evidence as proof that material hasn't been received unless the insurer has information to suggest otherwise (ICOB 6.2.6G).

Are any contracts exempt from the rules?

Certain contracts escape the requirement to provide the cancellation rights set out in ICOB 6. They include certain shorter-term policies such as:

■ travel insurance or similar contracts with a period of cover of less than one month;
■ pure protection contracts of six months or less that are not distance contracts; and
■ connected contracts that are not distance contracts.

Connected contracts are: those covering the breakdown of or damage to non-motor goods supplied by the provider; and those covering damage to, or loss of, baggage and other risks linked to travel booked with the provider (see Chapter 5).

What information should customers receive about cancellation rights?

The insurer should give each retail customer information about their cancellation rights in a durable medium in accordance with ICOB 5 (see section V). Customers, in other words, should be informed of:

- the existence of the right to cancel;
- the duration of the cancellation period;
- the consequences of not exercising the right to cancel; and
- how the right to cancel may be exercised.

Where the required information has been provided, the insurer need not accept a notice of cancellation if it is served later than the period specified.

What is the effect of exercising the right to cancel?

By exercising the right to cancel under ICOB 6, the retail customer withdraws from the contract. The insurer must refund any money paid no later than 30 days after notification of cancellation. In some cases the insurer may retain certain reasonable costs incurred in providing services to the customer before cancellation.

VII Claims handling (ICOB 7)

The purpose of ICOB 7 is to ensure that claims are handled fairly and settled promptly. Customers must be provided with information on the claims handling process and an explanation of why a claim is rejected or not settled in full. As stated in section II above, ICOB 7 also contains rules on how insurance intermediaries must disclose and manage conflicts of interest.

Again, the rules in ICOB 7 need to be considered in the context of PRIN, in particular Principle 6 (which requires a firm to pay due regard to the interests of customers and to treat them fairly) and Principle 8 (which requires a firm to manage conflicts of interest fairly). They also need to be read in the context of the FSA requirements for effective systems and controls (SYSC in the FSA Handbook).

Who does ICOB 7 apply to?

The insurer is responsible for claims handling and remains responsible if any claims handling is outsourced (including where it gives an intermediary authority to handle claims on its behalf). Certain rules do, however, apply to intermediaries who act on behalf of the customer (see below).

The bulk of ICOB 7 covers claims made by retail customers; only part of it applies to claims by commercial customers.

ICOB 7.6, which deals with motor vehicle insurance, extends to claims representatives appointed in EEA states outside the UK to handle claims for injuries sustained in accidents in other EEA states.

What are the rules for handling claims?

When handling claims made by commercial customers, insurers must:

- act fairly and promptly;
- provide guidance to assist customers in making a claim;
- keep customers 'reasonably informed' of how claims are progressing; and
- pay promptly once settlement terms have been agreed.

The insurer must not unreasonably reject a claim made by any customer (see below).

Specific additional obligations for handling claims made by retail customers include:

- responding promptly to notifications of claims and providing certain information on the claim;
- keeping the customer reasonably informed about progress of the claim;
- notifying customers as soon as practicable whether or not the claim has been accepted (in full or in part) and explaining the reasons for the decision; and
- settling promptly claims accepted by the insurer.

What are the rules for third-party claimants?

Where the insurer deals directly with a third party who claims against the insurer's customer but bypasses the customer to claim directly against the insurer (e.g. in the case of certain motor claims), ICOB 7 does not require the insurer to treat the third party as a customer (although it should not deal with the claim less favourably than it would have done if the claim was made against its customer).

What are the rules for rejection of claims?

Insurers must not unreasonably reject a claim made by any customer (commercial or retail).

They must not, unless there is evidence of fraud, refuse to meet a claim made by a retail customer on the grounds of:

i)   non-disclosure of a fact material to the risk that the retail customer could not have been expected to have disclosed;
ii) misrepresentation of a fact material to the risk (unless the misrepresentation was negligent); or
iii) breach of warranty or condition, unless the circumstances of the claim are connected with the breach.

These requirements echo the old Association of British Insurers (ABI) Statement of General Insurance Practice.

What are the duties of intermediaries?

The rules in ICOB 7.4 apply to insurance intermediaries and reflect certain common law duties owed by insurance intermediaries to their customers. When acting for a customer making a claim, insurance intermediaries:

i)   must proceed with due skill, care and diligence; and
ii) must not, in connection with any claim, put themselves in a position of conflict of interest unless they can manage the conflict by disclosure and by obtaining customers' consent.

Conflicts of interest are almost inevitable where the intermediary who has arranged a policy for the customer then handles claims for the insurer. In such circumstances, the intermediary has a duty to inform the customer it is acting for the insurer and obtain the prior informed consent of the customer. However, disclosure and consent may not, of themselves, be enough to reconcile the conflict of interest; in cases like this, the intermediary may have to stop acting for one or both of the parties.

VIII   Distance non-investment mediation contracts with retail customers (ICOB 8)

When does ICOB 8 apply?

ICOB 8 is applicable to insurance intermediaries who agree to provide a retail customer with ongoing services in relation to general insurance and pure protection policies by a remote means (e.g. post, fax, e-mail, telephone, internet).

ICOB 8 will not apply if the intermediary sells an insurance contract to a retail customer on a one-off basis, even if the intermediary is involved in the renewal of the contract and handling claims under it.

ICOB 8 will also not apply if the intermediary makes it clear in its terms that, in conducting its mediation activities, it acts on behalf of the insurer not the customer.

The FSA says it expects ICOB 8 to be relevant in 'a small minority of cases'. It will only apply if both of the following conditions are met:

i) an insurance intermediary concludes a distance contract with a retail customer for supply of insurance mediation services that are *additional* to any insurance contract it is marketing; and

ii) the distance contract has a 'life of its own' – i.e. independent continuity – and is not entered into merely in the course of effecting other business.

To sum up, ICOB 8 only applies where the distance non-investment mediation contract is of some kind of permanent nature and is not ancillary to or a by-product of other insurance business.

What are the rules in ICOB 8?

An overview of some of the rules is given below.

Disclosure requirements

In good time, before the conclusion of the distance non-investment mediation contract, the insurance intermediary must provide the retail customer with the full terms of the contract in a durable medium and comply with the status disclosure requirements set out in ICOB 8.

The status disclosure requirements are more numerous than those for other general insurance contracts to reflect the requirements of the EU Distance Marketing Directive (see Chapter 11, page 117).

There are certain exemptions to the requirement to provide the prescribed information *before* conclusion of the contract. These include: telephone sales; where the customer *requests* the contract to be concluded by a means of distance communication (other than the telephone) and it is impracticable for the intermediary to supply all the information required in a durable medium beforehand.

Restrictions on unsolicited services

Unsolicited services (i.e. services that a retail customer hasn't requested or consented to) in relation to a distance non-investment mediation contract are prohibited if they include requests for immediate or deferred payment or enforce any obligation on the customer. Absence of reply does not constitute consent. The rule against unsolicited services does not apply to tacit renewals of distance non-investment mediation contracts. See Chapter 13, section III.

Cancellation requirements in respect of distance non-investment mediation contracts are summarised separately in ICOB 8, but they reflect the ICOB 6 requirements for cancellation. A retail customer will have 14 days to cancel the contract, starting from the day the contract is concluded or the day they receive the terms and conditions etc in a durable medium – whichever is the later.

The other Conduct of Business Rules

The ICOB Rules are joined in the FSA Handbook not only by the Conduct of Business Rules for investment contracts (**COB**) but by a third module, **MCOB** or Mortgage Conduct of Business, which covers the sale and distribution of regulated mortgages.

COB formed the lengthiest (by number of pages) module in the whole of the FSA Handbook, running to more than 800 pages. The FSA has described the rules as 'increasingly difficult for users to navigate and understand – and therefore comply with'. In late 2007, COB will be replaced by a new version which will implement a more principles-based approach to regulation of the conduct of business.

Although the structure of the COB module is similar to that of ICOB, the rules are very different. They are, for example, far more prescriptive about details that have to be supplied about certain products. One consequence has been a move in investment advertising towards emphasis on brand rather than product.

An explanation of COB and MCOB is outside the scope of this book. The important point to note is that knowledge of all three sets of

Conduct of Business Rules may be required. If, for example, a customer is applying for a mortgage to buy a house, but is also sold an endowment policy to repay the mortgage, and payment protection insurance against accident, sickness or unemployment, then all the modules – COB, MCOB and ICOB – would be relevant.

5

The secondary insurance market

This chapter deals with organisations that are involved in the sale and distribution of insurance products, but whose main line of business is something else. These organisations are often known collectively as the secondary market.

Who's in the market?

The promotion and sale of insurance products is no longer the exclusive province of the businesses traditionally associated with it, such as insurers and insurance brokers. Many other companies and organisations have recognised the potential of insurance products to make money.

Banks and building societies have appreciated that they can profit from their standing as respected financial services providers by selling (or permitting the sale of) a wider range of financial services and products. Many retailers and utility providers have realised the potential to market financial services products, including insurance, to their existing customers. Property managing agents and freight forwarding companies are often involved in arranging insurance in the course of their other business. Charities have realised that 'diversification' into insurance might be a way to increase funds; pet charities, for example, offer insurance for pets. Since only an insurance company authorised by the FSA (or a friendly society or a Lloyd's syndicate) can underwrite insurance, these 'secondary market' organisations must team up with insurers to offer insurance products to customers.

Often the alliance will be known as an 'affinity' or 'corporate partnership' arrangement. In many affinity arrangements there is an inherent link between the insurance product and the core business of the partner. Sales of pet insurance by vets, or of home insurance by mortgage lenders, flow naturally from the primary activities of those businesses and it may be relatively easy to achieve a policy sale in the course of another transaction. Similarly, a car dealer may include the sale of motor insurance and warranty insurance in the process of selling a car, and a department store that is signing up a customer to a store card may find the customer is willing to take out credit insurance.

Sometimes, however, the link between the seller and the policy or product isn't obvious; insurance product ranges offered by corporate partners are tending to expand. Companies are realising that where their brand is strong people might be prepared to buy insurance products unrelated to their primary area of business.

What's in it for insurers?

This route to the market has a number of benefits for insurers. First, through their partner they will be able to use customer lists that include details of consumers they might otherwise not be able to access. If the corporate partner has a strong brand, they may be able, by using that brand to endorse the insurance, to attract those who don't usually buy insurance. For example younger consumers might buy insurance endorsed by a football club or mobile phone company.

Further, the corporate partner may be able to carry out some of the marketing, sales and even claims handling activities on behalf of the insurer. This provides the insurer with an infrastructure without the involvement of its own staff. An insurer will typically only pay for the services of a partner that sells policies on its behalf through commissions on policies sold. This reduces financial risk, since the insurer only has to pay the producer of the business for 'done deals', and is not required to invest capital in the venture.

There may be other practical advantages. Where the corporate partner is itself authorised by the FSA, it will be directly responsible to the regulator for policy sales, so will relieve the insurer from much of the work of ensuring the day-to-day compliance of the activities carried out by the partner. It must, however, be remembered that an insurer can never escape regulatory responsibility by outsourcing its activities in this way: the FSA has made it clear in its guidance that a regulated firm cannot outsource its own regulatory requirements.

How does FSA regulation affect the secondary market?

As we have seen in Chapter 2, the FSA regulates various activities in relation to the marketing and sale of insurance policies, as well as assistance in the administration and sale of insurance. Authorisation from the FSA is required before these activities can be conducted. You cannot arrange insurance or make arrangements with a view to insurance contracts, advise on the merits of buying cover or deal in insurance contracts as agent for the insurer or the policyholder unless you are either authorised by the FSA to do so, or are the appointed representative (see page 56) of a firm that has the relevant FSA permissions.

If a shop selling store credit cards wishes to introduce its customers to an insurance company for the sale of credit insurance, it is likely to be carrying on the regulated activity of making arrangements with a view to contracts of insurance. A retailer that went further than this and signed customers up to insurance cover in store with the authority of an insurance company would be likely to be carrying on the regulated activity of dealing in insurance as agent of the insurer.

In some circumstances, however, activities that would otherwise be regulated may be carried out without FSA supervision. This is because the rules allow for a number of exclusions.

What exclusions are available to secondary intermediaries?

Below we look at the exclusions most frequently relevant to the activities of secondary intermediaries.

Connected contracts – travel insurance (Article 72B Regulated Activities Order)

In the run-up to FSA regulation of the general insurance market, the government was lobbied by travel industry bodies such as the Association of British Travel Agents (ABTA), which argued that travel agents would be sufficiently regulated through ABTA's own code of conduct. The government was persuaded by these arguments to introduce an exclusion, though the situation is under review in 2007.

Any activity by a supplier of travel-related services in relation to a 'connected contract of insurance' is excluded from regulation by the FSA.

The most obvious beneficiary is a travel agent selling travel insurance along with a holiday, but the exclusion could also be available to other businesses where other travel-related services are sold. For example, it could apply when an airline sells a flight, or where a business arranges car hire or accommodation.

In order for suppliers to qualify for the exclusion, the travel insurance must satisfy a number of conditions. Essentially, they will only be excluded if:

a) the policy is not a contract of long-term insurance (that is, it does not provide life assurance or similar cover);
b) the total duration of the policy is five years or less;
c) the annual premium is €500 or less, or the equivalent amount in sterling or other currency;
d) the policy covers the risk of damage to, or loss of, baggage and other risks linked to the travel booked with the supplier;
e) the insurance does not provide cover in respect of the liability of the insured person to third parties except where that cover is ancillary to the main cover provided by the contract;
f) the insurance is complementary to the service being provided by the supplier; and
g) it is of such a nature that the only information that a person requires in order to carry on the insurance mediation activities is the cover provided by the contract. The FSA considers that this condition is likely to be satisfied where the insurance contract is a standard form, the terms of which (other than the premium) are not subject to negotiation.

The exclusion only applies to the supplier of the travel services, and not to anyone else who may be in a contractual chain between the supplier and the insurer, such as another intermediary from whom the supplier may source the cover. It does not exclude travel insurance policies from the requirement that they be underwritten by an authorised insurer.

As noted above, ABTA members are subject to their own code of conduct, and this regulates their sales of travel insurance. In recognition of the high standards the industry will need to demonstrate under the review, ABTA put in place a two-stage certified examination process. All ABTA members must ensure that all staff selling or offering insurance have passed a Level 1 exam, and at least one person in each office a Level 2 exam.

Despite this pre-emptive strike from ABTA, consumer groups and some MPs have argued that a lack of FSA regulation of the sale of packaged travel insurance has left the public exposed. Launching its review in August 2006, HM Treasury acknowledged such concerns and set out to:

- establish an evidence base to develop a better understanding of any significant problems in this market;
- consult widely with stakeholders, with particular reference to the scale and nature of any consumer detriment; and
- consider the options for regulating the sale of travel insurance as part of a package – including that of supervision by the FSA.

Connected contracts – non-motor goods (Article 72B Regulated Activities Order)

The government was also persuaded to introduce an exclusion for activities by a supplier of non-motor goods in relation to a 'connected contract of insurance'.

Typically, this exclusion will be available to a supplier of goods who wishes to offer extended warranty cover. Like the travel exclusion, it only applies if certain conditions are met. The following are broadly similar to those for travel insurance, though there are some differences:

a) the policy is not a contract of long-term insurance (that is, it does not provide life assurance or similar cover);
b) the total duration of the policy is five years or less;
c) the annual premium is €500 or less, or the equivalent amount in sterling or other currency;
d) the policy covers the risk of breakdown, loss of, or damage to, non-motor goods supplied by the provider;
e) the insurance does not provide cover in respect of the liability of the insured person to third parties;
f) the insurance is complementary to the non-motor goods being provided by the supplier; and
g) it is of such a nature that the only information that a person requires in order to carry on the insurance mediation activities is the cover provided by the contract. As noted above, the FSA considers that this condition is likely to be satisfied where the insurance contract is a standard form, the terms of which (other than the premium) are not subject to negotiation.

As with that for travel cover, this exclusion only applies to the supplier of the goods and not to any other parties who may be in a contractual chain between them and the insurer. It does not exclude warranty insurance policies from the requirement that they be underwritten by an authorised insurer; see Chapter 6 for when warranties are classed as insurance contracts.

The government's decision to introduce this exclusion was in large part based upon a 15-month inquiry by the Competition Commission in 2002 (including a public hearing) into the supply of extended warranties on domestic electrical goods in the UK. The Commission concluded that a complex monopoly situation existed in the market for extended warranties, which operated against the public interest, and proposed a package of remedies. This was accepted in whole by the government and implemented in the form of the Supply of Extended Warranties on Domestic Electrical Goods Order 2005. Under the order retailers must:

■ show the price of the extended warranty alongside electrical goods, in store and in their printed advertising material;
■ provide consumers with information about their statutory rights, cancellation rights and details of the warranty, including whether or not the warranty provides financial protection in the event of insolvency and terminates if a claim is made;
■ give consumers 45 days to cancel the extended warranty, providing them with a written reminder of this right and the right to receive a refund; and
■ offer quotations to any consumer who does not wish to buy a warranty immediately, stating that the extended warranty remains available on the same terms for 30 days if the consumer chooses not to buy it at that time. (Any discounts tied to the purchase of the extended warranty must also be available for 30 days.)

The decision to exclude insurance warranties for domestic goods from FSA regulation is subject to review in 2008.

Provision of information on an incidental basis (Article 72C Regulated Activities Order)

This exclusion does not apply to all regulated insurance mediation activities – only to the arranging activities and the activity of assisting in the administration and performance of insurance contracts. It excludes any activities that:

a) consist of the provision of information to the policyholder or potential policyholder;
b) are conducted by a person in a profession or business that does not otherwise consist of regulated activities; and
c) amount to the provision of information that may reasonably be regarded as being incidental to that profession or business.

Several important points should be noted. First, the exclusion only extends to information given to the policyholder or potential policyholder and not to the insurer. Thus, an intermediary who forwards a proposal form to an insurance undertaking would not qualify for it. Similarly, where a person does more than provide information (for example, by advising a customer, or helping a potential policyholder fill in an application form), they would be seen as carrying on a regulated activity.

In the FSA's view, to be 'incidental', the activity must arise out of, be complementary to or be otherwise closely connected with the profession or business. In other words, there must be an inherent link between the activity and the company's main business. A simple example, given by the FSA, is that of a dentist: if they introduce dental insurance, they may benefit from the exclusion; if they introduce pet insurance, they do not. In addition, the activity must not amount to the carrying on of a business in its own right.

The exclusion applies to a person whose business does not otherwise 'consist of' regulated activities. In the FSA's view, the fact that someone carries on regulated activities in the course of a business (and may be authorised by the FSA in respect of them) does not, of itself, mean that the business *consists of* regulated activities. If the main focus of your profession or business is something else and the criteria (a) and (c) above are met, you should qualify for the exclusion.

The fact that this exclusion applies to those whose core business is not insurance mediation makes it particularly relevant to secondary intermediaries. It is, however, important to remember its limited scope. It will be necessary to look at the activities of an intermediary in a proposed corporate partnership carefully; they could mean the exclusion won't apply. In some cases, it may be possible to tailor the activities to fit the exclusion; much will depend on the commercial deal between the parties.

Enabling parties to communicate (Article 27 Regulated Activities Order)

This exclusion does not apply to all regulated insurance mediation activities – only that of making arrangements with a view to contracts of insurance. It provides that a person does not carry on the activity of making arrangements with a view to contracts of insurance *merely by providing means by which one party to a transaction (or potential transaction) is able to communicate with other such parties.*

This means that businesses such as internet service providers or telecommunications networks are excluded if all they do is provide communication facilities. The FSA says that the word 'merely' is crucial and, where a publisher, broadcaster or internet website operator goes beyond what is necessary for them to provide their service of publishing, broadcasting or otherwise facilitating the issuing of promotions, they may well bring themselves within the scope of the making arrangements activity. So while this exclusion may be of relevance to a corporate partner who simply arranges links or other advertising on its website for an insurer or other intermediary, it is necessary to consider the particular circumstances carefully.

The FSA outlines situations in which a publisher, broadcaster or website operator who is carrying banner advertising from another intermediary or insurer, or who sets up links to their websites, would be unlikely to be able to use this exclusion. It takes the view that the exclusion is unlikely to be available where, as part of the arrangements, the person concerned does one or more of the following:

a) brands the investment service or product in their name or joint name with the broker or product provider;
b) endorses the service, or otherwise encourages readers or viewers to respond to the promotion;
c) negotiates special rates for their readers or viewers if they take up the offer; and
d) holds out the service as something they have arranged for the benefit of readers or viewers.

The FSA also says that the exclusion probably won't apply if the person concerned earns commission based on the amount of regulated business done as a result of the promotion. The existence of the financial interest will inevitably affect how the purpose of the arrangements is seen.

It should also be noted that when dealing with advertising materials, the FSA's financial promotion rules are likely to apply: see Chapter 4. These should therefore be considered in addition to the question of whether authorisation is needed.

Claims management for an insurer (Article 39B Regulated Activities Order)

Under this provision, among other things, claims management for a 'relevant insurer' is excluded from the activity of assisting in the management and performance of a contract of insurance.

A 'relevant insurer' includes most insurers, but there are some minor exceptions (for example, an insurance company which underwrites certain limited types of motor breakdown cover for which FSA authorisation is not required).

Claims management for policyholders is not covered by this exclusion and is therefore a regulated activity within the assisting activity.

Appointed representatives

How does the arrangement work?

As we have seen in Chapter 2, when an authorised person makes someone an appointed representative, they agree to be responsible to the FSA for all the activities of the AR within the scope of the appointment. As far as the FSA is concerned, it is as if the acts and omissions of the AR were made by the AR's principal or appointer. For this reason, AR status is likely to be attractive to an intermediary whose involvement in insurance is limited and who does not wish to take on the considerable compliance burden of authorised status. For the same reason, insurers or other intermediaries are often reluctant to appoint ARs, preferring not to take on the additional burden of ensuring the compliance of their partner in carrying out their insurance-related activities and the risk involved in being responsible for the partner's compliance.

Some insurers may have an internal policy against AR appointments; for others, the decision whether to appoint an AR in a particular case may be a question of balancing the benefits from the partnership against the compliance burden involved.

There are two types of AR: what might be termed a 'full' AR and what is referred to in the FSA Rules as an 'introducer' AR. The latter is one whose appointment is limited to introducing customers to providers and distributing promotional materials. The FSA regime for introducer ARs has a slightly lighter touch than that for full ARs.

What's the due diligence process?

The principal has specific obligations before making an AR appointment. In summary, they must check the suitability of the AR, that it is ready and organised to comply with the relevant rules and (except where the appointment is of an introducer AR) that it is solvent. Once the appointment has been made, the principal is required to monitor these matters, and if there are problems, to take immediate steps to rectify them, or terminate the appointment.

What must the AR contract include?

Wherever an AR is appointed, the FSA Rules require there to be a written agreement between the principal and the AR setting out the terms of the appointment and incorporating certain mandatory terms. A summary of these appears below.

Required contract terms for all ARs:

- either prohibit the AR from carrying out certain regulated activities for other parties; enable the principal to impose such a prohibition; or restrict the other parties for whom such activities can be carried out or the types of investment involved;
- prohibit the AR from carrying out business pursuant to the appointment unless the AR is included in the FSA's register for that purpose;
- require the AR to comply with FSMA and FSA Rules in carrying out the regulated activities for which it is appointed and to make sure that anyone providing services to it (including employees) also complies;
- require the AR to notify the principal if it is seeking appointment as the AR of any other firm, with details of that firm and the activities concerned, and of any change in the business concerned or the termination of any such appointment; and

Additional required contract term for introducer ARs:

- to limit the scope of the appointment to effecting introductions to the principal or members of its group and distributing non-real-time financial promotions relating to products or services available through the principal or other members of its group. (Non-real-time financial promotions include written or broadcast material but do not include those made during the course of a personal visit, telephone conversation or other interactive dialogue.)

When drafting an AR agreement, the principal will probably wish to go beyond the required terms set out above and include others to protect its position, such as indemnities in respect of contract breaches, service standards and appropriate termination rights in the event of default and other circumstances.

Contracts between insurers and intermediaries: general principles

Whenever an insurer and another party enter into a partnership, there should be a written contract setting out the commercial deal and the other terms governing the legal relationship. This is essential from a risk management perspective; indeed, the FSA is likely to take the view that an insurer or authorised intermediary that did not enter into a written agreement with its business partners was not fulfilling its systems and controls obligations (see Chapter 3).

We deal in Chapter 7 with the principles of agency, which often form the legal basis of the relationships between insurers and intermediaries. The precise structure of the agreement may be influenced by the parties' intentions in relation to branding. For example, where the product and sales process are to be 'white labelled' and the partner's brand is to take prominence over that of the insurer, it may be intended that the insurer or another party should conduct sales activities in the name of the partner. FSA rules requiring parties dealing with customers to disclose their identity and status (see Chapter 4) may present difficulties with this and may dictate the contractual structure.

The terms that should be included in a distribution agreement are numerous and will vary according to the precise nature of the deal in question. For example, each party is likely to wish to deal with the requirement for the other to obey FSMA and the FSA rules. Where the intermediary is to act as agent for the insurer or other party, the agreement will need to set out the scope and limits of the agency (see Chapter 7 for more details). Where one party is using the other's brand or other intellectual property, there will need to be provisions that grant a licence to do so (see Chapter 11). Where an outsourcing transaction involves the transfer of staff such that the TUPE Regulations may apply, the parties may wish to agree what the consequences will be: see Chapter 13.

Where the distribution agreement involves material outsourcing, there are particular terms that should be put in place according to FSA rules: see Chapter 10. Similarly, certain terms are mandatory in agreements between principals and appointed representatives (see page 57).

Distribution deals are commonly on an exclusive basis. The insurer may wish to prevent its partner from selling the products of other insurers; the partner may wish to ensure that the insurer does not sell competing products. The parties will need to consider (and the agreement will need to reflect) the duration and scope of any exclusivity: to whom should exclusivity apply and what products or markets should be covered? Any exclusive arrangements should also be considered from a competition law point of view. (see Chapter 12).

In this book we concentrate on aspects of the contract which relate particularly to insurance distribution deals. There are, of course, many other, more general issues to consider when putting together the contract.

The parties will need to consider practical matters such as the circumstances in which the agreement may be terminated, how notices are to be given, and (where foreign countries may be involved) which country's legal system is to apply to the contract. Is there anything (such as premium rating information or business methods) that needs to be kept confidential to the parties? How will disputes between the parties be resolved: by public court proceedings, by mediation or by arbitration? Should any third parties have any rights under the contract? In Chapters 8 to 13 we deal in more detail with certain of the key legal provisions that need to be considered when putting insurance distribution agreements in place.

6

Inadvertent breaches of the law

It is possible to enter into an arrangement that constitutes insurance without realising it. The corollary is that commercial organisations are sometimes guilty of inadvertent breaches of the laws that regulate the insurance industry in the UK.

As explained in Chapter 2, there are criminal sanctions and implications for the enforceability of contracts if inadvertent breaches have been made. Avoiding liability depends, in large part, on an understanding of how insurance is defined in UK law.

This chapter explains the main characteristics of regulated insurance and how the law is likely to decide borderline cases. It also looks at the position of those who distribute insurance on behalf of a foreign company or whose policies include products underwritten by others. (See the boxes on pages 65 and 66.)

What is insurance?

It is an important question, but one that is not easy to answer. Much of the difficulty arises from the fact that there is no definition of insurance in

FSMA. It is necessary to refer to previous decisions of the courts to understand what insurance is for the purposes of the law.

Helpfully, the FSA has issued guidance summarising its views on the principles established by case law, in particular by the leading case of *Prudential v Commissioners of Inland Revenue* (1904). This is to be found in Chapter 6 of the 'Perimeter Guidance' (PERG) issued by the FSA as one of the Regulatory Guides.

FSA guidance does not bind the courts but it might influence a court considering whether it would be just and equitable to allow a contract to be enforced (see Chapter 2).

If a person acts in line with its guidance, the FSA will proceed on the basis that they have complied with its requirements. In other words, the person will be unlikely to be prosecuted or disciplined.

On the basis of case law and the FSA's guidance it is possible to state the basic characteristics of insurance. An arrangement is likely to be insurance if it comprises:

a promise by one party to pay money to or confer some other benefit on another on the happening of an uncertain event that is adverse to the recipient's interests in return for payment.

Taken together, the elements of an insurance contract described above involve a transfer of risk from the insured to the insurer, who agrees to deal with the consequences if the uncertain event occurs. This transfer of risk is the essence of insurance. We will look at each of the elements in turn.

The insurer's promise

Usually, under the terms of an insurance policy, the insurer will promise to pay money to the insured if a 'what if' (an 'uncertain event') becomes a reality. For example, under a fire insurance policy, the insurer will agree to pay the costs of rebuilding a property if it is damaged by fire. Under a solicitor's professional indemnity policy it will agree to pay the cost of defending a claim against the solicitor by a client and any damages for which the solicitor is liable.

Sometimes, the amount payable will not depend on an assessment of the damage or loss suffered by the insured; instead, a pre-agreed sum will be paid. This is common in accident insurance; such a policy may provide, for example, that the insurer will pay £500 if the insured breaks an arm or £10,000 if they lose an eye. The principle in each case is the same: to compensate for the event insured against.

However, insurance need not involve payment by the insurer; instead, the promise may be to confer some other benefit. An example of this is motor breakdown insurance (such as that offered by motoring associations to their members). In this case, the insurer agrees to give assistance to the motorist if their car breaks down, by recovering the vehicle, providing alternative transport, attempting emergency repairs etc.

The uncertain event

The uncertainty is often over *whether* an event will happen. The type of breakdown policy just discussed provides for assistance to be given *if* the car breaks down. In some kinds of insurance, however, the uncertainty is over *when* the event will occur. The most obvious example is life insurance that pays out *when* the insured dies. Life insurance, though, is beyond the scope of this book.

The uncertain event must be adverse to the interests of the insured. This is what essentially distinguishes insurance from gambling: under a gambling contract, there is an agreement by one party to pay another on an uncertain event (for example, Arsenal beating Manchester United in the FA Cup Final), but there need be no connection between the other party and the event and it need not be adverse to their interests (they do not need to be a Manchester United player or supporter to place the bet).

The payment

In general, there must be some payment by the insured for the insurer's promise, in keeping with the general legal requirement for every contract to involve 'consideration'. However, it is also possible, as with any type of contract, for insurances to be executed as a deed, in which case contract law does not require consideration. It is also important to note that where cover is said to be 'free of charge' to the consumer, it is likely that someone (for example, a retailer making a promotional offer) will have paid for it. The fact that cover is free to the consumer does not prevent its being insurance or within the FSA regime.

The timing and amount of the payment are relevant. If it is reasonable to conclude that there is a genuine pre-payment for services to be rendered in response to a future contingency, the contract is unlikely to be one of insurance. In the FSA's view this requirement will be satisfied when there is a commercially reasonable and objectively justifiable relationship between the amount of the payment and the cost of providing the benefit. Contracts for the periodic maintenance of goods, whether or not a breakdown or failure has occurred, are unlikely to be insurance.

What happens in borderline cases?

In borderline cases, it may be possible to avoid regulation by structuring an arrangement so that it is not classed as insurance under FSMA. The substance of an arrangement, rather than its form, is more important in deciding whether it is insurance. It's not enough simply to avoid the language of insurance – terms such as 'cover' or 'premium'. You have to think of what the arrangement *means.*

Below we look at how some borderline cases have been treated in law.

Discretionary schemes

In the case of *Medical Defence Union Ltd v Department of Trade* (1979), the court decided that a scheme operated by the Union for its members did not constitute insurance. Under the scheme, doctors and other medical staff can request assistance with their defence if they're sued by patients. Crucially, though, the request is granted at the *discretion* of the Union; no *promise* is made to give it; there is no obligation on the part of the Union.

The court found that the benefit under a contract of insurance had to be 'money or money's worth'; the members of the Union had a right to be considered for assistance, but this was not money or money's worth. The court reached its decision even though there was evidence that assistance was rarely refused. According to FSA guidance, it may be the case that such a contract is not insurance even if, in practice, the provider has never refused a benefit.

This case provides a good illustration of the nature of the provider's obligation in a contract of insurance. The court noted, though, that making benefits discretionary is not likely to be an easy way to sidestep the requirement for FSA authorisation. Most customers will not be interested in schemes that only give them a right to be considered for an indemnity if a claim arises.

Warranties

Warranties for goods purchased by consumers are a tricky area. In the simpler cases, the purchase price includes an amount for repairs or replacement if a defect emerges within a defined time after purchase.

Under statute law, terms regarding quality are implied in a contract for the sale of goods or services. Consequently, the FSA's guidance indicates that it is unlikely to regard a manufacturer's or retailer's warranty as insurance if it does no more than crystallise or recognise obligations of the same nature as the seller's or supplier's usual obligations.

In other cases, a warranty may be provided by a person other than the seller or supplier of the goods, or may be significantly more extensive in content, scope or duration than the seller's or supplier's usual obligations. When this happens the FSA is likely to view the contract as a contract of insurance.

It should also be noted that where a third party is providing a warranty that constitutes insurance, the seller or supplier will, as an intermediary, need to be either appropriately authorised by the FSA or an appointed representative (see Chapters 2 and 5).

Tax investigation schemes

Tax accountants who complete self-assessment returns for their clients often agree to deal with any enquiries or investigations that may be carried out by HM Revenue and Customs (HMRC) once their work is done. In return, their clients pay them an annual fee.

Some providers have argued that such agreements are equivalent to a 'manufacturer's warranty' in respect of the accountants' own work and therefore should not be treated as insurance in law. The FSA, however, disagrees. It takes the view that these schemes are likely to be insurance contracts because they cover the client not just when the quality of the provider's work is in question but also when the HMRC makes random checks.

The FSA's position has implications for other arrangements. It could, in theory, apply to any proposal to provide services as and when they are required in return for an annual fee.

Disaster recovery schemes

It is common for disaster recovery providers to agree to provide a customer with priority access to information technology (IT) and related facilities in the event of an occurrence that causes a business-critical system to fail. Such agreements do not, according to the FSA, constitute insurance. In the cases it reviewed, it found providers did not guarantee access to the replacement facilities, but offered them on a 'first come, first served' basis. This meant that there was no relevant assumption of risk by the provider; it could enter into numerous such contracts without increasing the probability of its resources being inadequate to meet all claims.

The FSA also found that the total fees charged to the customer bore a reasonable and justifiable relationship to the commercial cost of the services actually provided. Fees were levied after the emergency facilities were used and calculated according to level of use.

Distributing the products of foreign insurers

What are the rules?

The FSA regime only governs activities that are being carried on in the UK. The laws of other countries regulate insurance-related activity within those jurisdictions. Problems may arise when an insurance transaction has a cross-border element.

If there is any possibility that insurance business will be carried on overseas (for example, because policyholders or insured property are located there), it is necessary to consider the laws and regulatory system of the country concerned. Those are outside the scope of this book.

By the same token, foreign insurers need to take great care to ensure that they have the necessary FSA authorisation if they are doing business in the UK. The leading case of *Re Great Western Assurance Co SA* (1999) illustrates the point. Although the case pre-dates FSMA, it can still be seen as representing the law; the statutory framework at the time was similar to that provided by FSMA.

In the *Great Western* case, overseas insurers underwrote insurance policies with UK-based insured parties. All underwriting decisions were taken in the insurers' own jurisdictions and claims were paid from accounts located in those jurisdictions. Brokers in the UK performed various functions on behalf of the insurers, including selecting risks to refer to the insurers within guidelines agreed with them, making recommendations to the insurers about what risks to accept, receiving notification of claims by policyholders on behalf of insurers, instructing loss adjusters and settling claims below a specified amount. This was consistent with then current practice, as the understanding prevalent at the time was that as long as underwriting decisions and claims payments were made offshore, an insurer would not be considered to be carrying on business in the UK.

Nonetheless, the court decided that the activities by the brokers on behalf of the insurers amounted to carrying on insurance business in the UK. It found that the business of an insurer is not simply limited to making underwriting decisions and paying claims but also includes other preparatory or ancillary activities.

It was important to the court in this case that the brokers' activities were carried out regularly and systematically on behalf of the insurers. Even so, it can be concluded that you don't have to do *that* much to be seen as doing insurance business in the UK. Do little but do it regularly and systematically and you'll fall within FSA jurisdiction.

What are the implications?

Any business planning to make arrangements to distribute an insurer's products in the UK needs to make sure the insurer has FSA authorisation. It will not avoid the UK regulatory system by simply ensuring that the contract is made overseas.

For insurance companies established elsewhere in the EU, obtaining FSA authorisation is a relatively simple process. Essentially, this is because the EU is committed to the principle of the free movement of services and establishment between member states. An insurer authorised by the regulator of its home state and wishing to carry on insurance business in another EU country is entitled also to be authorised by the regulator of the proposed host state, subject only to certain notification and other requirements. Such an authorisation is known as a 'passport' and it entitles the 'bearer' to provide services in another EU state or establish a branch – or do both.

For insurers outside the EU, there is no short cut to FSA authorisation and a full application is required.

Restrictions on insurers' activities

Just as there are rules, set down by case law, for what is and what isn't insurance, so there are rules for what insurers can and can't do. Insurers, in other words, operate within a set of boundaries.

FSA authorised insurers are subject to a rule (at 1.5.13R of the Prudential Sourcebook for Insurers in the FSA Handbook, abbreviated to INSPRU) that restricts their commercial activities to insurance business and the things that arise directly from it (the rule is a little different for insurers whose business is restricted to reinsurance). The purpose of this rule (which was introduced into UK law to comply with European directives regulating insurance business) is to give further protection to policyholders. If insurers diversify they take on increased financial risks and this could materially affect their ability to pay claims when due.

'Insurance business' in this rule means the business of effecting or carrying out contracts of insurance as principal. The rule restricts the insurer to those activities that arise directly from their **own** underwriting business. This has clear implications for arrangements with other insurers. As the FSA puts it, in order to act as intermediary in relation to the products of other insurers, an insurer must show a 'natural fit and necessary connection' with its own products.

The rule can cause problems for those insurers that wish to offer other products as additional benefits in their policies. Often, the 'add-on' will be provided by another company – for example, legal expenses cover in a motor or home insurance policy. In these circumstances, it will be necessary to be able to justify the decision to include the additional benefit by reference to the rule in the Integrated Prudential Sourcebook (PRU).

Alternatively, potential solutions include arranging to route the sale of policies through another group company that is not an insurer. That company would, of course, have to be an authorised intermediary or an appointed representative of a party with the appropriate FSA permissions.

7

Principles of agency

As will be clear from earlier chapters, the distribution of insurance products in the UK often involves or relies on the use of an intermediary – a middleman between the underwriter and policyholder. This makes agency law an important issue for the insurance business. This chapter looks at how, and when, it may be applied.

What constitutes an agency in law?

A contract of agency is a relationship between two parties where one, the 'agent', is considered in law to represent the other, the 'principal'. The agent in an insurance context will typically be an insurance broker (acting for either an underwriter or a policyholder), but that need not be the case. Other parties in the distribution chain may take on the role of agent – for example, corporate partners selling underwriters' products (see the box on page 78).

A key factor of the relationship is the ability of the agent to bind the principal to contracts with third parties by acts that the agent is said to have the principal's *authority* to perform.

The scope of the agent's authority will vary from relationship to relationship. And it will be open to interpretation; this is not a straightforward area of the law (see the section on authority below).

Probably the most important legal principle to bear in mind is that agency is a question of *fact*. A number of terms can be indicative of agency relationships – e.g. 'binder', 'delegation', 'agency', 'representative', 'broker', 'intermediary', 'consultant', 'coverholder' and 'material outsourcing' – but none is conclusive. Terminology tells us nothing about the agent's authority to bind; whether and to what extent an agency relationship has arisen is determined in law by what was in fact said and done, by whom and in what context.

What are the agent's rights and obligations?

In establishing rights and obligations under agency agreements and deciding whether breaches have occurred, the courts will take the following into account:

a) the scope of the agent's retainer/express terms;
b) implied terms; and
c) market practice (though this will be harder to establish, and therefore a less important factor, in corporate partnerships).

The scope of the retainer/express terms

This refers to the spoken and written instructions of the principal to the agent: what has been expressly asked for by the principal and what the agent has agreed to do. Agency law is closely allied with contract law, but the extension of an agent's retainer does not require a contractual variation – an agent's authority may be extended (including orally) after written contracts have been executed.

Until relatively recently, it was rare for brokers to enter into detailed written arrangements with clients. They have, however, now recognised the importance of recording agency arrangements in writing and will tend to enter into terms of engagement (with an insured) and terms of business or delegated/binding authority agreements (with an insurer). In other words, express terms are now usually easier to discern.

The scope of an agent's legal duties may also depend on the type of principal – its level of experience/sophistication. Where, for example, the principal is a relatively inexperienced policyholder for whom a broker is handling a claim, the broker may be reasonably expected to do more than merely comply with instructions. The courts have held that an insurance broker must make use of their knowledge of the market and use appropriate skills (*The Zephyr*

(1984)). In other words, in acting as agents, brokers cannot expect to rely solely on the instructions of the other party; their role is not passive; it is not simply about 'obeying orders'.

The same principle can apply, in part at least, when the agency is between a broker and an experienced insurance professional. In 1997, National Insurance & Guarantee Corporation sued brokers Russell Tudor Price for failing to ensure that reinsurance policies allowed it to recover loss of interest on the use of its own funds. The court held that the brokers had been negligent. The judge conceded, however, that an experienced professional like the reinsured should have spotted the defect and therefore reduced the brokers' liability by 30 per cent. (There have been more recent examples that have shown that brokers are expected to go beyond merely following instructions – even for a fairly experienced client.)

Implied terms of agency

Common law duties

As with all contracts of service, the agent has an implied duty to carry out its services with reasonable skill and care. What is 'reasonable' was established by *Bolam v Friern Hospital Management Committee* (1957). The 'Bolam test' means that a person who has held himself out as capable of attaining standards of skill is required to show the skills normally possessed by persons doing that work.

'Reasonable standards' can vary with circumstances, but, generally speaking, the following will be true: agents said to be in breach of duty will be judged by the standard of their peers; and the more complex the issue and the greater the claim of expertise by the agent, the higher the expected standard.

An agent is bound to carry out its principal's instructions. Where no time-frame is stipulated in a contract, the instructions should be carried out with 'reasonable' dispatch. Again, what will be considered 'reasonable' will depend on the circumstances; an agent will be under a general duty to keep its principal informed of developments.

If an agent fails to meet the expected standards and is sued for negligence, the claimant will need to show that it has relied on the agent to carry out the duty alleged to be owed. And that reliance must be 'reasonable'. (This applies to all claims against professionals.)

Fiduciary duties

The nature of the relationship means that an agent has fiduciary obligations to its principal. The practical impact of this is that it has, by law, a duty to observe safeguards that protect the principal.

In return, the principal protects the agent from liabilities incurred in carrying out its instructions and acting on its authority. It might, for example, indemnify the agent against the costs of defending a claim against it by a policyholder.

To fulfil its fiduciary duties, the agent must:

- be trustworthy;
- act in the principal's best interests;
- not make a secret profit (i.e. one that is not disclosed to the principal);
- not put itself in a position where its interests and those of another for whom it acts conflict (or may conflict) with the interests of its principal (if there is such a conflict, the agent will probably have to stop acting for both parties);
- make full disclosure of all material information to the principal;
- not use a principal's property for personal gain; and
- respect confidentiality.

When these duties are breached, the principal has the right to either rescind the contract of agency or affirm it and demand a return of all profits made. Which course of action it takes will depend very much on the particular circumstances – not least the status of a distribution arrangement at the time the breach occurs.

Market practice

Market practice may be considered a fair indicator of what is 'right and proper' or acceptable in agency relationships. For a market practice to be recognised by the courts, it will need to be well known (and widespread), certain and reasonable. Market practice will be less relevant where a detailed written contract sets out the agent's obligations.

What determines the scope of the agent's authority?

Unless properly defined and identified by a contract, the scope of the agent's authority is likely to be in dispute. Exactly what is the agent authorised to do on behalf of the principal? And are the acts of the agent within the scope of its authority? These are the kinds of questions that cause difficulties.

The situation is made more complex by the fact that, in order to protect the policyholder or customer, different kinds of authority are recognised in law. An agent can have both actual and perceived authority to act on another's behalf. The latter category includes the concepts of 'actual' and 'ostensible' authority and 'agency by estoppel'.

Actual authority

As indicated at the beginning of the chapter, a relationship of agency is created when a principal confers upon another power to enable them to execute a particular task. It naturally follows that the principal will be bound by the acts of the agent within such authority. This is known as the 'actual authority' of the agent.

Actual authority consists of both the express (written or spoken) authority of the principal and an *implied* authority to carry out any necessary or incidental acts to effect the task for which authority has been given – to put it another way, the minutiae of performing the particular task. The actual authority of the agent (both express and implied) limits the scope of the arrangement between principal and agent. However, it's only half of the picture.

Perceived authority

This is the other half. It is not uncommon for a third party to be misled into thinking that an agent has authority when it doesn't. For this reason, the law also recognises that a third party may be entitled to regard an agent as having the requisite authority to carry out a particular task because of something said or done by the principal. This is the concept of apparent authority; the idea that an agent can appear to a third party to have *greater* authority than it actually does.

A related (but different) concept is agency by estoppel. This arises where an agent appears to have authority to act but in fact has *no authority at all*. Estoppel is a doctrine applied in several areas of law and exists to protect a third party who relies on information or advice given to them by a supplier of services. An insurer who tells an insured that a policy won't be cancelled for late payment of premium could be estopped from cancelling, if, for example, the insured as a result has not arranged alternative cover.

The doctrines of apparent authority and agency by estoppel operate as a function of what others reasonably perceive and in this sense can be characterised as the external perception of authority; it does not matter what state of affairs *actually* exists between the agent and the principal. Nevertheless, it should be borne in mind that in cases of both apparent authority and agency by estoppel the perception must arise from words or conduct that amount to a clear and unequivocal representation to the third party originating (in some sense) from the principal. This might be express or implied (for example, expected from previous dealings).

Apparent authority is sometimes also called – or considered to include – 'ostensible' authority. This is the 'usual authority' that a third party can expect to take for granted in dealing with an agent in the normal course of business. In other words, it is dictated by the current customs of the marketplace. A third party may, for example, reasonably assume a claims handling agent to have the authority to accept notification of claims.

It is worth remembering that while agency can be terminated at any time, the apparent authority of the agent may continue after its actual authority has been revoked. Therefore, any contract entered into with an insurer after the agent's actual authority ends will be valid if the customer does not have notice of the termination.

What happens when an agent acts outside its authority?

Ratification

The principal may, subject to various limitations, choose to ratify 'unauthorised' acts/contracts. Ratification, in this sense, is also regarded as a type of actual authority. Ratification can be effected expressly or implied.

Express ratification will involve the proposed principal confirming orally or in writing that they are treating a contract as valid and that they are the actual principal. (The contract will be valid from the date it was made, rather than the date of ratification.)

Implied ratification occurs when the principal behaves in a way that suggests unequivocal adoption of the contract (for example, paying a claim or receiving a premium, suing on the policy or defending a claim on it, retaining monies paid).

A delay in repudiating the agent's authority could ratify the agreement. Ratification will, in particular, be inferred where the proposed principal knows that the third party is acting on the basis that the contract is in full force and yet does nothing to disabuse them of the false premise on which it was made. In these circumstances, the principal could be estopped from denying that they are bound.

It should also be noted that, if adopted, the contract will apply in its entirety: a principal cannot ratify only a part of any contract.

Legal action

As we saw in Chapter 5, an insurance intermediary must either be authorised by the FSA or be the appointed representative of an authorised business (or be able to claim an exemption or exclusion).

When a regulatory breach occurs, an agent may be subject to FSA censure and a policyholder may have recourse to the Financial Ombudsman.

However, neither the regulator nor the ombudsman can intervene to protect the insurer from the commercial consequences of the agent's mis-selling. It is the insurer, not the agent, who will be liable for any loss suffered by the third party. Crucially, this applies whether the agent's authority is actual or apparent.

In cases of apparent authority or agency by estoppel there are, however, certain preconditions for liability. Representation by the principal must:

i) have been communicated to the party with whom the agent contracted;
ii) be relied upon by that third party;
iii) be the proximate cause of the belief that the agent was authorised to act;
iv) justify the inference that the third party knew of and relied upon it in entering into the contractual relationship; and
v) have been made intentionally or recklessly.

In some circumstances, the insurer principal will have a claim against the agent for exceeding its authority. If it does, and it intends to pursue it, it must proceed with care. In many cases, ratification of a contract with a policy-holder will constitute a waiver of the agent's breach of duty. Principals should check that sufficient procedures are in place to protect their rights to pursue the agent.

What should contracts cover?

This section looks at some of the key issues for agency agreements and at some of the things that should be borne in mind when contracts are being drawn up. It is not a detailed examination of contract terms.

Giving advice

It is vital for an agent to refrain from giving advice on subjects outside its expertise. If the principal's instructions are simply to offer certificates of insurance in certain limited circumstances, the agent should not, for instance, invite trouble by telling people that the insured is 'adequately covered'.

The principal should make sure appropriate restrictions, caveats etc. are included in the agency agreement. It might, for example, want to stipulate that points that fall outside either party's area of expertise are checked, or, if it's a multinational, that advice is restricted to the position in the UK.

The law will impose a duty of care on an agent giving advice. This will be difficult to discharge if they don't really know what they're talking about.

Remuneration

Entitlement to remuneration for services rendered will depend on the express or implied terms of the agency contract. Where there are express payment terms, then those terms will apply. Payment will otherwise be determined by any terms that may be implied into the contract by a court. The court will consider all the circumstances of the case and, unless there are good reasons not to, 'award' the agent reasonable payment.

Subject to any express terms to the contrary and a few exceptions imposed by law, a court will imply terms that an agent has the right to be reimbursed for all expenses and to be indemnified against all losses and liabilities incurred in the execution of its authority. The agent could also be entitled to a reasonable sum for any services not covered by the agency contract, but freely accepted by the principal.

The agent will not be entitled to remuneration for:

i)   any unauthorised transaction (not ratified by the principal);
ii) breaches that go to the root of the contract;
iii) unlawful acts.

As stated in the section on fiduciary duties above, an agent must not make its own profit from the contract (unless the principal consents to such an arrangement). Part of the purpose of an agency relationship (particularly a corporate partnership) will be to assist the other party, not compete with it. An agent should not therefore take its own undisclosed profit from the insurer's business. And it should not 'offer, give, solicit or accept an inducement' that is likely to conflict to a material extent with duties owed (ICOB, Rule 2.3.2).

Commission can be paid on whatever basis the parties agree e.g. monthly, quarterly or annually. It can be payable on the placement of a policy or following settlement of a claim. There is plenty of scope for a principal and agent to agree on what is most commercially suitable. However, care must be taken to ensure compliance with the FSA's commission disclosure rules (see Chapter 4).

Another common feature of an agent's remuneration arrangements is permission to set off the amounts of any expenses, losses or liabilities against sums due to the principal (unless the money due to the principal is held on trust). In the event of cancellation or avoidance of a policy, the insurer is liable to pay the gross premium (or applicable part thereof) to the policyholder but is not entitled to claw commission back from the agent (unless otherwise agreed).

Acting for more than one principal

An agent is obliged not only to ensure it doesn't make a secret profit from the principal's business or give or receive an unfair inducement but also that it is in a position to act in a full and frank manner. This may not be possible where it acts for more one than principal.

If a conflict is perceived to exist, it is essential that the agent obtains the principal's fully informed consent before acting for another.

Interestingly, English law does not recognise the concept of a pure intermediary, that is, someone who acts for two parties concurrently, to the satisfaction of all concerned. The courts invariably find that an entity is acting as the agent of one party or another in any given context.

However, in some circumstances, an insurance agent can act in a dual capacity – i.e. for both the insurer and the insured. Perhaps the most obvious example is where a broker is instructed by a customer to obtain cover from an insurer and the broker has a separate delegated authority from the insurer to effect the cover. Another example is where the broker is instructed to obtain a survey or loss adjuster's report.

In acting for two parties, the agent's overriding obligation is to make sure the interests of one do not conflict with the other – i.e. that its position is not compromised.

Delegation of duty to sub-agents

In a typical broking situation, the insured will be expected to understand that the broker may appoint sub-agents, and the authority of the principal to sub-delegate may be implied – particularly if the principal is aware that the agent intends to sub-delegate its authority or where the contract *depends on* the use of sub-agents. (It is relatively common for the principal in a corporate partnership arrangement to permit, in certain circumstances, the appointment of sub-agents.)

It must be stressed that the dominant presumption in law is that the sub-agent is responsible to the agent and not to the principal, and that the authorisation of a sub-agency by the principal does not automatically create a contractual relationship between it and the sub-agent. (A direct relationship between principal and sub-agent generally only exists for the purposes of holding funds – see Chapter 9.)

In the absence of a contractual relationship with the principal, the agent should be liable for the sub-agent's breach of duty. The corollary is that the principal cannot sue the sub-agent for breach of contractual obligations – these are owed to the agent.

The principal need not remunerate or indemnify the sub-agent. By the same token, the sub-agent cannot be held responsible to the principal for monies had and received, even though these are ultimately intended to reach the principal.

The difficulty of establishing a contractual relationship as far as a sub-agent is concerned will more often than not be reinforced by the presence of a clause that excludes the Contracts (Rights of Third Parties) Act 1999. Under that Act, any entity that is not party to the contract (for example, a sub-agent), but on whom a contract 'confers a benefit', could be entitled to assert rights. Only in very rare circumstances will the agent and principal not want to exclude the Act from the contract of agency, as not doing so can give rise to uncertainty.

While the position under contract law is clear, some confusion surrounds the principal's rights to sue a sub-agent for breach of fiduciary duty or make a claim in tort. In practice that sort of claim is likely to be difficult.

Managing the risks of agency relationships

Summary of the risks

A contract of agency has the potential to damage the brand/and or reputation of the insurer and affect its financial standing. The main reasons for this are given below:

i) the agent may systematically exceed underwriting authority – e.g. by offering insurance that is outside the terms permitted by the agency agreement;

ii) there may be no effective remedy against the agent or, indeed, the principal (e.g. in cases of insolvency);

iii) it can be relatively easy for the policyholder to establish the agent had apparent authority;

iv) the Financial Ombudsman is not obliged strictly to observe the legal preconditions for apparent authority listed on page 74, in cases of uncertainty the Ombudsman may find for the policyholder; and

v) an agent could act for a number of principals and conflicts of interest could therefore arise.

Summary of risk mitigation

To a large degree, the risk profile and management of risk will depend on the partner identified. It is essential, therefore, that an insurer selects and appoints an agent with care.

The next stage is to write a clear and sufficiently detailed agreement. Once this has been signed, all parties should ensure that proper risk management protections and procedures are in place to avoid any disputes about what could or should (not) have been done by any agent. This will mean:

- regularly reviewing procedure and personnel;
- ensuring that the parties are receiving and producing the right management information at the right intervals;
- ensuring that independent audits are carried out regularly (and there is a right to terminate the agency agreement if an entity fails an audit);
- ensuring that all amendments to the initial written agency relationship are approved by the right people (e.g. the legal and compliance teams) and that all such amendments are made in writing and then signed off by someone of sufficient seniority (or a 'reserve' person in their absence); and
- ensuring that each party has a remedy in the event of a complaint or breach.

NB Specific and detailed information on managing the risks of intermediary insolvency appears in Chapter 9.

Agency law and corporate partnerships

Corporate partnerships are explained in detail in Chapter 5 on the secondary market. They are relatively new arrangements, and exactly how the courts will analyse them is currently unclear. However, lawyers expect the agency principles established in the majority of broker cases to apply in a similar – if not equal – way.

In a corporate partnership, an agency relationship will usually be clearly set out in a written agreement between the agent and the principal, and the express terms will be clearly defined.

Implied terms may include a duty to do more than passively follow the insurer's instructions. Insurers will usually select a corporate partner on the basis of its ability to carry on insurance business effectively and professionally (or, before effecting an appointment, require systems and controls to be put in place by the intermediary to ensure professionalism). It is likely, therefore, that, in a corporate partnership context, an intermediary would be expected to use its market knowledge and appropriate skills. The courts have recognised brokers as professionals (see page 70) and may decide to treat professional agents in a distribution deal in the same way.

The principles of market practice that have been established in cases relating to brokers should act as a useful guide for entities in a corporate partnership.

Pricing and remuneration

This chapter deals with what may be termed the 'mechanics' of a typical distribution agreement between an insurer and intermediary. It explains how insurance products are priced, how premiums are collected and when refunds will be made. And it discusses the different methods of paying intermediaries: commission; advances; profit-sharing; fees.

I Pricing insurance products

What's the 'system'?

In most cases, it will be the insurer who has the right to set the selling price of the insurance products. If so, the insurer will usually agree to pay the intermediary a percentage of the selling price, after the deduction of any applicable Insurance Premium Tax (IPT), as the intermediary's commission.

It is possible for the selling price to be determined by the intermediary. In this case, it is likely that the insurer will have the right to set the net premium rates. Based on these, the intermediary will set the selling price of the insurance products. The difference between the net premiums and the selling price (after the deduction of any IPT) is usually retained by the intermediary as its commission.

For a brief explanation of IPT, see the box on page 91.

What factors influence prices?

The selling price of the insurance products can be fixed for the duration of the distribution agreement. However, it's more likely that it will fluctuate – in line with circumstances. Some of the factors that will determine prices (and changes in prices) are looked at below.

Competition

Both the insurer and the intermediary will be keen to ensure that the products are priced *for the marketplace* – in other words, that they're going to sell. There are many methods that intermediaries and insurers use to ensure that prices are competitive. They include:

Review meetings
The insurer and the intermediary may agree to meet regularly and review sales performance. If things aren't going well, the insurer may decide to reduce the premiums and/or the intermediary may decide to reduce its commission.

A review meeting may be called when a conversion target is not met. If fewer customer enquiries are being converted into sales than expected/desired it could be because the price is too high; the parties will need to meet to discuss what action to take.

Benchmarking
The parties may agree that the premiums payable for the insurance products will be compared with those payable for competing products – either regularly or as circumstances demand.

The scope of the benchmarking exercise will need to be quite carefully defined to ensure like-for-like comparisons. In deciding on the 'comparator group', the parties will need to think about the following:
i) *Policy benefits.* Are the products truly similar to those under review? Insurance products of the same type may contain different benefits (for example, the cover provided by different payment protection policies may be subject to different financial limits).
ii) *Sales channels.* How are the products being distributed? Insurance is sold through a variety of channels (e.g. by telephone, over the internet, by intermediaries or by insurers selling directly to the public), and different channels have different 'cost profiles'.
iii) *Promotions.* Are the prices of the products 'true'? The sellers of an insurance product may decide to make promotional offers for a limited period in order to stimulate sales. This may be done, for example, by discounting the price of the product by a set percentage or offering free cover during the first few months of the policy.

'Special offer' prices do not represent the prices that would normally be payable for products. Therefore, the parties may wish to exclude discounted products from the benchmarking exercise.

Profitability

The parties will make assumptions about:

- sales volumes – the number of products sold;
- claims costs – the number and value of claims;
- expenses – the costs incurred in selling and administering the products (from call-centre and claims handling costs to the costs of reinsurance and FSA compliance).

They will then determine the level of profit they need to make and set prices accordingly.

However, it's possible (likely even) that one or more of their assumptions will prove wrong. Sales performance may be better or worse than expected; costs and expenses may be higher or lower. If this happens, there will be commensurate rises and falls in profits, and the parties will probably wish to set prices again.

Profitability can be affected by regulatory and legal change. FSA and other legal requirements may vary during the course of the distribution agreement; as may the way that the parties are taxed. The parties may want to recover any additional compliance expenses and/or taxes incurred during the life of the agreement through price increases.

Marketing

As indicated above, the parties may wish to try to stimulate sales through promotions such as special or introductory offers.

What are the disclosure rules for pricing?
Under the ICOB Rules, both retail and commercial customers must be provided with price-related information (see Chapter 4, page 39). In addition, depending on the circumstances in which the insurance product is being sold, there may be other statutory requirements for the disclosure of pricing – for example, under the Supply of Extended Warranties on Domestic Goods Order 2005 and the Consumer Credit Act 1974.

Paying for promotions

The way price promotions are to be funded will need to be discussed and then set out in the distribution agreement. The parties may wish to 'split the difference' equally – i.e. each receive a proportionate reduction in the amount of money made on the insurance products – or agree that only one of them will be hit. (Where the parties offer free cover for the first two months of an insurance policy, it may be decided, for example, that the insurer will receive only ten-twelfths of the annual premium but still pay the intermediary commission on the *full* annual premium for the insurance policy.)

The parties may agree to take a generic approach or, alternatively, that they will decide on the method of funding case by case.

II   Receiving and refunding premiums

What's the process for collection?

The insurer and the intermediary will need to agree on a process for receiving payments from policyholders. In doing so, they will need to think about the following.

Who's responsible?

The parties will need to decide whether the insurer will collect premiums from policyholders or whether they will be collected by the intermediary and passed on (usually after deduction of the intermediary's commission).

Regulatory implications

Premiums received by the parties will need to be handled in accordance with the FSA's client money rules. (These are discussed in detail in the next chapter.)

Payment methods

Premiums can be paid either in 'one go' or by instalments. The parties will need to decide on the right method for them; much will depend on the type of insurance being sold (the premium for single-trip travel insurance, for example, is usually paid upfront).

The parties may want to let the customer decide how to pay. It should be noted, however, that the option to pay by instalments may amount to the provision of credit and therefore be governed by the Consumer Credit Act 1974.

Insurance Premium Tax

In addition to the premium, the parties will need to collect from the policy-holder any IPT due – see page 91.

When do insurers make refunds?

In broad terms, refunds are made to policyholders when regulatory and legal requirements and market practice demand it.

Regulatory and legal requirements

The relevant provision includes ICOB, the Financial Services Distance Marketing Regulations 2004 and the Unfair Terms in Consumer Contracts Regulations 1999.

By virtue of ICOB, a customer who has been sold insurance by a 'remote' means (e.g. telephone, post or the internet) has the right to cancel the contract within a 'cooling-off' period – usually 14 days. If they do so, the insurer is legally bound to repay any premium within 30 days. (See Chapter 4 for further information.)

The Unfair Terms in Consumer Contracts Regulations have recently been used by the FSA to challenge the use in payment protection policies of clauses that prevent the payment of refunds on early repayment of the loan to which the insurance relates. Where refunds are offered, it has also challenged the way they are calculated.

As a result of FSA intervention, it is expected that insurers will have to offer premium refunds when the loan to which a payment protection insurance policy relates is paid off early.

Market practice

The parties may wish to refund a premium even where there's no legal requirement to do so. The rationale will be standard market practice; in other words, what competitors do and what's the accepted 'norm'. (In the field of motor insurance, for example, it appears to be standard for an insurer to refund premium to someone who cancels their policy early.)

What's the system for paying refunds?

The agreement will need to state whether the insurer is to pay refunds directly to policyholders or via the intermediary.

The insurer will be keen to ensure that it also expressly provides that, in the event of a refund, it can recover – or claw back – a proportionate amount of the commission paid to the intermediary who sold the policy. (In the absence of such an express provision, the insurer may not be able to recover commission.)

III   Paying intermediaries

What are the rules for commission?

Basic structure

Insurance distribution contracts will usually give the intermediary the right to receive commission on products sold.

As indicated above, the commission will often be the difference between the selling price of the insurance product and the net premium retained by the insurer. In situations where the intermediary determines the selling price, the level of commission earned per product is accordingly within its control. (The intermediary is unlikely to inflate the selling price to unrealistic levels as this would affect sales volumes and, ultimately, the total commission earned.)

In situations where the premium is controlled by the insurer, the commission is more usually expressed as a percentage of the selling price.

Another commission structure, sometimes adopted for high-volume and relatively low-premium products (for example, travel policies) is for the intermediary to earn a specified fixed amount per product sold.

Disclosure of commission

The rules for the disclosure of commission have been discussed in Chapter 4 (see page 38). The key point to bear in mind is that they cannot be looked at in isolation; they dovetail with the principles of agency law.

An intermediary acting as agent for a customer in securing cover with an insurer has fiduciary duties to that customer. These include the duty not to make a secret profit. Commission will be deemed to be a secret profit if it exceeds the market norm – i.e. if it's above what the customer might reasonably expect.

There has been no guidance from the courts as to what would constitute an appropriate level of commission; or as to whether this question will be looked at across the market as a whole or by reference to specific classes of business. However, in cases where intermediaries are earning particularly significant levels of commission (which will often be the case for creditor insurance and extended warranty insurance products), the intermediary could be at risk of making a secret profit if disclosure of the commission is not made to the customer at the outset.

If secret profits are made, money may have to be repaid to the customer.

Payment of commission

In cases where the intermediary collects the premium on behalf of the insurer, the intermediary will deduct its commission before passing the net balance of the premium and the IPT to the insurer. In cases where the premium is paid direct to the insurer, the insurer will usually forward the intermediary's commission at an agreed interval (often monthly).

Insurers will often stipulate that in the event that a policy is cancelled or otherwise fails to run for the expected period, the intermediary should repay to the insurer the pro rata proportion of commission already received. As seen above, this is known as commission clawback.

Volume-based commission

Intermediaries are sometimes entitled to additional levels of commission to reflect the overall volume of business underwritten – in layman's terms, to a kind of 'bonus'. This type of arrangement is distinct from the profit-sharing structures considered below.

Although volume-based commission arrangements (sometimes known as overriders) are not prohibited, their inclusion in insurance distribution arrangements should be carefully considered. The structure adopted must not put either party in breach of Principle 8 of the FSA's Principles for Businesses (Managing Conflicts), or the more specific ICOB Rule 2.3.2 in relation to unfair inducements (see Chapter 4).

What are the rules for 'advances'?

The insurer will sometimes agree to make an upfront payment to the inter-mediary when the distribution agreement is signed. If it does, the following will be important considerations.

Purpose of payment

If the advance is for a specific purpose (e.g. to fund IT development or marketing costs incurred by the intermediary), the insurer may wish to see it 'ring-fenced' – i.e. to prohibit its use for anything else.

VAT implications

The parties will need to consider whether the payment will be liable for VAT. This may depend on whether it is advance commission or made in return for marketing services provided by the intermediary.

Repayment on early termination

The parties will need to think about what will happen to the advance if the contract comes to a premature end. They may wish the agreement to stipulate that it will be repaid whatever the reason for the termination – or (more likely) only under specified circumstances. (The intermediary will probably argue that there should be no refund if it has terminated the contract because it's been breached by the insurer.)

Unfair inducements

The advance must not be structured in a way that conflicts with the unfair inducement rules. Care is needed if the advance might be seen as a disguised commission; the danger is greater if the amount of advance is dependent on meeting volume or business targets.

The ICOB Rules prevent the giving and receiving of any payment that may conflict to a material extent with the interests of customers. Examples of unfair inducements are given in Chapter 4.

What are the rules for profit sharing?

Basic structure

The intermediary will often negotiate the right to share in the profits generated by the insurer on the business sold under the distribution agreement. Profit-sharing arrangements are common in higher-value corporate partnerships and other affinity distribution arrangements.

An appropriately structured profit-sharing arrangement enables the intermediary to share in the profits of the underwriting venture without carrying any of the underwriting risk. (Losses will, though, be taken into account when assessing the intermediary's entitlement, as discussed below.)

From the insurer's perspective, profit sharing is a way of incentivising the intermediary to perform at the optimum level and to maximise sales.

Profit-sharing arrangements are typically included in a schedule to the main distribution agreement and will usually be structured around a formula that, in turn, will frequently be negotiated and drafted by the insurer's and intermediary's respective actuarial/finance teams. In more complex profit-sharing arrangements, there will also usually be quite substantial legal input to ensure that the parties' intentions are clear.

At the heart of all profit-sharing arrangements is a basic structure that involves the calculation of a net profit figure – the income received by the insurer, less agreed deductions (see below) – and the distribution of the money to the insurer and intermediary in an agreed ratio (for example, 50 : 50).

The starting point in structuring any arrangement is agreeing the period to which the profit-share calculation is to be applied and the corresponding frequency of distribution of any monies to which the intermediary may be entitled. Perhaps the most common structure involves an annual calculation.

Typically, intermediaries will press for relatively frequent calculations and distributions, with insurers preferring a longer lead time so that a more realistic picture of the profitability of the business can be built up. In motor insurance distribution agreements, for example, where the risks are relatively high, it is not uncommon for there to be a single profit-share calculation and distribution at the end of a five-year term.

Calculating the profit

The insurer's income

In most profit-sharing arrangements, the income included in the calculation will principally be premiums for business sold by the intermediary during the agreed period. It will be important to specify whether the income to the insurer is to be calculated on the basis of earned or written premium (or some other basis); and then to ensure that a consistent accounting treatment is applied to the deductions. Sometimes, the insurer will also allow investment income (i.e. interest earned on premiums received) to be included.

It's possible that reinsurance recoveries will form a separate element of the income stream. It's more usual, though, for these to be taken into account when total claims costs are calculated – see reinsurance costs, below.

The deductions

Commission – Commission that the intermediary has either received or is entitled to.

Claims costs – Typically, the actual or net cost to the insurer of settling claims: the indemnity paid to the insured and associated costs such as loss adjusters' and lawyers' fees.

IBNR – A reserve for claims 'incurred but not reported' and for claims that may prove to have been insufficiently reserved will also typically be included as a deduction.

Reinsurance costs – Insurers will often be able to deduct the cost of buying specific reinsurance protections (or a pro rata amount where the reinsurance covers more than the business sold under the agreement). Where such a deduction is agreed, the insurer would ordinarily be expected to give credit for reinsurance recoveries. It could do this either by classing the money paid out under the reinsurance policy as a distinct income stream or by deducting it from the figure for total claims costs.

Levies – Insurers are required to make payments, calculated as a specified percentage of premium income, to fund the FSCS. The proportion of this levy that relates to income generated by the distribution agreement will ordinarily be deducted by the insurer.

Insurer's return – This is the insurer's 'guaranteed' return on the business underwritten in the distribution agreement. The insurer will typically be entitled to retain this as its own profit and will therefore include as a deduction an agreed percentage of the total premium income.

Management costs – Sometimes, the insurer will be permitted to deduct management expenses.

Other features of profit-sharing arrangements

Transparency/control of profit-share calculation
As most of the information needed for the profit-share calculation will be within the control of the insurer, it will sometimes be agreed that the intermediary has the right to review the documentation that supports it. Related clauses in the agreement will specify a mechanism whereby the insurer's figures can be challenged.

Resolution of disputes
Any disagreement over profit-share figures will usually be resolved by a commercial discussion, held in the context of a known escalation procedure. Where differences remain, it may, however, be necessary for the parties to engage in a more formal dispute resolution process. Although the distribution agreement will provide for resolution either through the courts or arbitration, the parties may prefer 'expert determination'.

Asking an expert such as an independent actuary to decide the issue will usually be quicker, cheaper and less confrontational than court or arbitration proceedings – and therefore less likely to damage an ongoing commercial relationship.

Separation/aggregation of different lines of business

A distribution agreement will sometimes relate to more than one class of insurance business; home, motor and travel insurance are, for example, typically combined. Where this is the case, the insurer and intermediary will need to agree whether there are to be separate profit-share calculations and distributions for each – or some form of aggregated profit-share calculation for all.

Insurers will often prefer the aggregated approach. This is because it ensures that profits are only distributed to the intermediary when the performance of the entire book of business is good. The alternative has the potential to 'reward failure': the insurer may find itself distributing profits for two classes of business even though the third is doing so badly that the overall book is in the red.

Carrying forward losses

Where profit-share calculations are carried out reasonably frequently, say annually, and profit distributions made to the intermediary at similar intervals, it will sometimes be the case that a profit is paid for an underwriting period that ultimately proves to be loss-making. Typically, this happens when the calculation is based on actual claims costs and an assessment of IBNR that ultimately proves to be understated because of deterioration in the loss ratio. To protect themselves, insurers will usually provide that any adverse movement in prior year's claims costs/IBNR should be included as a further deduction in the calculation of subsequent years' net profits.

Unfair inducement

There must be a clear understanding between the parties that the intermediary is not being induced to mis-sell. That, in the quest for profits, they must remain fair to the consumer.

What about fees?

In traditional broking relationships, remuneration by way of fees for bespoke placements is becoming increasingly common. However, it remains fairly rare for volume retail business.

In some circumstances, the intermediary will be paid a fee in addition to commission. The obvious example is where an intermediary is contracted for activities such as claims handling as well as sales.

If fees are payable, the parties will need to consider whether they will attract Value Added Tax (VAT). This will depend on the type of activity to which the fee relates. A detailed analysis of the VAT position is beyond the scope of this book.

Insurance Premium Tax: the basics

IPT, a tax on general insurance premiums, is levied at two rates: a standard rate of 5 per cent; a higher rate of 17.5 per cent for travel insurance and some insurance for vehicles and domestic appliances.

Life insurance and most long-term insurance is exempted from the tax; as is reinsurance, insurance for commercial ships and aircraft and for commercial goods in transit. Premiums paid under policies covering risks outside the UK also escape – but they may attract similar taxes in other jurisdictions.

Source: HMRC

Funds held by intermediaries

Intermediaries routinely hold insurers' and policyholders' funds, for example, when collecting premiums, when handling refunds of premiums, or when handling claims. The risk for insurers and policyholders is that the intermediary might become unable to transmit those funds to the intended recipient – typically through insolvency.

This chapter focuses on how, in the field of general insurance, the risks to the policyholder are mitigated under English law. It also considers the tools an insurer might use to protect itself against loss of insurance money.

What are the rules?

I   Credit risk and agency law

The risks of fund holding can become additionally complicated where there is uncertainty over whether the relevant monies are held by the intermediary as agent for the insurer or as agent for the policyholder – in other words, over who actually owned the funds and who therefore suffers the loss as a result of the insolvency.

The factors that help determine whether an intermediary is acting as agent for the insurer or the policyholder at any given time have been considered in detail in Chapter 7, but if funds are held on behalf of the insurer, it is the insurer that bears the credit risk. This is the basic position in English common law.

It means that, where funds are held on behalf of the insurer:

1. If the intermediary has collected the full premium from the policyholder but becomes insolvent and unable to pass the money on, generally the risk will be with the insurer, even though it has received no payment for the policy.
2. If the intermediary receives funds from the insurer to settle a claim but becomes insolvent and unable to pay the policyholder, liability remains with the insurer. In other words, the principal is at risk of paying the claim twice: to its agent and again to its policyholder.
3. If the intermediary receives a policy refund payment from the insurer for transmission to the policyholder but becomes insolvent before the payment is passed on, the insurer remains liable to refund the policyholder; as in 2 above, it is at risk of double payment.

In each case, the insurer would have a legal entitlement to recover the relevant funds from the intermediary, but the likelihood would be that the intermediary would have insufficient assets to settle the debt. The general rule on insolvency is that unsecured creditors rank behind secured creditors. Once the latter have had their slice of the intermediary's assets, the remainder is aggregated and divided among all the unsecured creditors in proportion to their respective debts. Because an insolvent intermediary's liabilities would generally exceed its assets (often by a substantial margin), unsecured creditors would almost invariably receive substantially less than the full amount of the debt.

II   Chapter 5 of the Client Assets Sourcebook (CASS 5)

In 2005, when it became the watchdog for general insurance mediation, the FSA laid a new stratum on to agency law – Chapter 5 of the Client Assets Sourcebook (CASS 5). The implementation of CASS 5 has greatly reduced the risks to which the policyholder would previously have been exposed, while at the same time imposing onerous obligations on intermediaries to comply with the client money rules or alternatively on insurers to accept credit risk transfer.

The overriding principle of CASS 5 is that customers should be protected from the inability of an intermediary to transmit insurance funds; this could be in relation to premiums, refunds or claims monies. CASS 5 amplifies the provisions of Principle 10 of the FSA Handbook which states that, where a firm is responsible for a client's assets, it must arrange adequate protection for those assets.

What do the rules mean?

The FSA has produced the Guide to Client Money for General Insurance Intermediaries to help explain the application of CASS 5, setting out the regulatory position as at 31 March 2006. While the guidance is not formal and can, in the event of any discrepancy, be 'overruled' by the FSA Handbook, it is a useful source of further information on how intermediaries are permitted to receive and hold insurance monies.

CASS 5 has laid down two different routes for achieving the goal of consumer protection. Intermediaries must deal with insurance money by: transfer of risk from the client to the insurer; or segregating and holding on trust clients' money in client accounts.

The intermediary does not have to stick to one of the above methods: it is permitted to use different methods for different clients or for different transactions entered into for the same client.

Credit risk transfer and holding money as agent

Under the risk transfer mechanism, the intermediary holds insurance monies on behalf of the insurer; in other words, the risk of the intermediary becoming insolvent is transferred to the insurer.

When a premium is paid by the insured to the intermediary it *becomes* the insurer's money on receipt. By the same token, if agreed by the insurer and intermediary, when claims or premium refunds are paid by the insurer to the intermediary they *remain* the insurer's until received by the insured.

On an intermediary's insolvency, the insurer will be an unsecured creditor (unless it has independently put some form of security in place).

If the insurer and intermediary agree that insurance monies will be held in this way, a written agreement must be entered into stating that premiums (and, if applicable, claims and premium refunds) are held by the intermediary as agent for the insurer and that the intermediary is authorised to act for the insurer in receiving insurance monies.

Where there is an extended broker chain, CASS 5 places limitations on the extent to which credit risk transfer can apply: although sub-agents and intermediaries further down the chain are permitted to hold funds on a credit risk transfer basis, they may only do so if the insurer agrees that for the purposes of holding the relevant funds, there is a direct relationship of agent and principal between it and the intermediary. The objective is to make the legal relationships as simple as possible so that the consequences of an intermediary's insolvency become easier to deal with. A direct relationship of agent/principal for money would be unaffected by the insolvency of an intermediary higher up the chain, whereas if the monies were held in a sub-agency the insolvent agent's liquidator could have a claim to the funds.

There are further requirements for the parties to the agreement; in particular, the insurer must be satisfied that the terms of the applicable insurance policies are likely to be compatible with a risk transfer arrangement, and the intermediary must disclose the arrangement to clients who may be affected.

As the insurer is accepting the risk, the intermediary will generally not need the FSA's permission to hold insurance money in this way. If the intermediary intends to mix the money held as agent for an insurer with client money held in a non-statutory or statutory trust (see below), they must obtain the insurer's consent. This process is known as co-mingling.

The insurer's consent must subordinate the interests of the insurer to the interests of the customer and, if the funds are co-mingled, the funds held as agent for the insurer must comply with the requirements for client money held on trust as set out in CASS 5.3 to 5.6.

Trust and segregation of client money

The rules here are complex. At their core, however, are simple principles: the aim is to separate money that is rightfully the client's from that which is rightfully the intermediary's – or its creditors'.

Definition of client money

Client money will usually be money that an intermediary receives and holds on behalf of its clients in connection with insurance mediation activities.

As a general rule, monies held by the intermediary are not classed as client money where they are either the intermediary's funds, or are held by the intermediary on behalf of the insurer under the risk transfer method. The exception to this is where money is held on behalf of the insurer but the insurer has agreed in writing that the intermediary may treat the money as client money.

Monies will also not be client money if received under an arrangement whereby the intermediary delegates the mediation activities outside the UK to a third party – CASS 5.1.5R.

Where monies are held by an intermediary as agent for the policyholder the client money rules will apply – even if there is a chain of brokers between the intermediary holding the funds and the policyholder.

Client money accounts

Client monies must be segregated in client accounts: when the intermediary receives insurance monies from the insured or the insurer, the funds are held legally by the intermediary but *beneficially* for the insured or insurer. This creates a trust that protects the client monies from forming part of the intermediary's estate. It means that in the event of the intermediary's failure the money held in the client account will be distributed in a 'pecking' order:

- for insureds, according to their respective interests in the trust;
- for insurer clients, according to their respective interests in the trust;
- for payment of costs attributable to distributing the money; and, finally,
- for the intermediary.

NB This method does not confer complete protection to the insured. Unless the insurance policy states to the contrary, an insured party does not discharge its obligation to pay the premium to the insurer simply by paying the intermediary. If the intermediary fails before passing the money on, the policyholder may have to pay the premium again. The trust rules would, however, mean that they should have access to their funds so that they would ultimately avoid double payment.

Statutory and non-statutory trusts

Monies held in a client account will be held on either a statutory or a non-statutory trust basis. The statutory trust will arise automatically under the FSA rules unless a non-statutory trust is adopted by the intermediary.

The provisions of the statutory trust are very basic: client money is held on trust for clients and, if there is co-mingling, relevant insurers, in their respective proportions and for distribution in the order set out above.

The non-statutory trust model provides the possibility of greater flexibility, but also requires additional resources and processes. An intermediary may only adopt a non-statutory trust if it has:

- adequate systems and controls to ensure that it is able to monitor and manage its client money transactions;
- written confirmation from its auditors that it has such systems and controls (there is little guidance as to what would constitute adequate systems and controls);

- a designated manager to oversee the systems and controls;
- at least £50,000 in capital resources;
- informed consent from its clients to the non-statutory trust arrangements; and
- a formal deed setting out the terms of the trust.

The rules of CASS 5 permit the intermediary to include in the terms for a non-statutory trust an ability to give credit in respect of client money. This means that the intermediary can pay premiums *before* it is actually in receipt of funds from the client, and pay claims funds and refunds to the client *before* it has received funds from the insurer. (It is, though, forbidden from extending credit to itself in respect of trust monies – for example, by paying itself commission for any premium paid under the credit terms.)

Setting up client money bank accounts

As already stated, client money must be segregated from the intermediary's money. In practical terms, this means it must be held in a bank account separate from the intermediary's accounts. The account can either be a general client bank account or a designated client bank account. Designated accounts contain monies relating to specific clients or specific categories (e.g. different offices of a particular client) and will usually be set up at the request of the client.

Further information on setting up and maintaining client bank accounts is given in the box on page 101.

What are the methods for distributing client money in the event of insolvency?

The way clients recover money in the event of business failure somewhere in the supply chain varies according to circumstances and according to whether the funds were held in general or designated accounts.

Primary pooling

The main trigger for a primary pooling event is where the *intermediary* is insolvent. A primary pooling event will not occur where a third party or the bank becomes insolvent.

A primary pooling event will result in all client money in each of the intermediary's client accounts (general and designated) forming a common pool of money so that each client will only have a claim to the pool in general and not to a specific sum. In practical terms, this means that any shortfall between the money held for a client and the client's entitlements will be shared between all clients, and the client may not receive all of their funds back from the intermediary. If this is the case, the customer may make a claim against money held in the intermediary's own accounts; however, as they would probably be an unsecured creditor, the prospects of significant additional recovery would often be slim.

The primary pooling rules will not be applicable where the client money is received after the intermediary's insolvency. Such monies must be placed in a client money account opened after the event and held in accordance with the client money rules and, except where the monies relate to a transaction that has not been completed or are due at the time of the primary pooling event, returned to the client as soon as possible.

Secondary pooling

A secondary pooling event occurs on the failure of a third party to which client money held by the intermediary has been transferred. When client money is transferred to a third party, the intermediary continues to owe a fiduciary duty to the client; however, in accordance with general law, as long as the intermediary has complied with its fiduciary duties (whether as agent or trustee), it will not be held responsible for a shortfall in client money caused by a third party's failure. The intermediary may decide to make up any shortfall in the client money themselves; in which case, a secondary pooling event will not occur.

Failure of a bank

On the failure of a bank, all general bank accounts of the intermediary will be pooled, including all those held at other banks, and any shortfall will be borne by the clients holding money in the general bank accounts.

All designated bank accounts at the failed bank will be pooled and any shortfall will be borne by the clients whose money is held in them. This ensures that clients do not suffer from the loss of the bank that has failed unless they hold money in its accounts: designated accounts are only pooled where the bank that holds them is insolvent.

In a secondary pooling event, designated accounts will have no right to claim any monies in a client bank account of the intermediary.

Failure of a third-party broker or settlement agent

Where a third-party broker or settlement agent to whom the intermediary has transferred client money fails, all client monies in general client bank accounts of the firm will be pooled in the way they would be if a bank failed. This results in the unhappy outcome that all clients of the intermediary that are holding monies in a general client account will have to bear the shortfall of the sums paid to the failed broker regardless of whether that broker placed their insurance.

On the failure of a third-party broker or agent, client money held in designated accounts does not have to be pooled.

Does CASS 5 apply to reinsurance mediation?

CASS 5 specifically carves out intermediaries carrying out mediation activities in respect of reinsurance contracts. The intermediary may elect to comply with the client money rules in reinsurance contracts provided that it does so for *all* reinsurance business and keeps a record of the election.

What protection is available to the insurer?

The policyholder, as we've seen, is protected by stringent rules about what an intermediary can and cannot do with their money. What about the insurer? How can it protect itself?

Any insurer entering into a risk transfer arrangement should only do so if it is satisfied with the financial standing of the intermediary. Insurers can further mitigate the risk of losing insurance monies by limiting the amount of premiums the intermediary is able to hold at any one time. While this method is generally preferable for the insured, if the insurer becomes insolvent the insured will not be able to recover any premium, claims or refunds paid to and still held by the intermediary: this will be the insurer's money, which the intermediary will 'owe' to the administrator or liquidator. In addition, under this mechanism, the intermediary will not be obliged to obey the insured in any dispute over insurance monies as they act as the insurer's, rather than the insured's, agent.

From the insurer's perspective, the key is to ensure that, insofar as possible, in the event of intermediary insolvency, its assets are ring-fenced – or that some other form of valid and enforceable security is in place. From the intermediary's perspective, the key factors are cost and complexity: where an intermediary is dealing with a number of insurers, there can be many actual and opportunity costs associated with ring-fencing an insurer's money and/or providing security. Other forms of risk mitigation for the insurer are considered below.

Co-mingling

The insurer can allow its funds to be mixed with client money in the intermediary's client account. This has the advantage of trust law protection, but the downside is that the insurer must agree that its rights are subordinated to those of the intermediary's clients; if there is a shortfall in the client money account on insolvency, it is the insurer that is likely to take the hit.

Standby letters of credit and on-demand bonds

Under these, a bank agrees to pay a specified amount to the insurer on the happening of a specified trigger (i.e. non-payment of a debt). Standby letters of credit usually cost a percentage of the credit limit and are slightly more expensive than on-demand bonds.

Letters of credit and on-demand bonds have obvious advantages for the insurer: they are secure, easy and (relatively) cheap. The disadvantages are that the bank charges may affect the financial arrangements between the insurer and intermediary. Also, the bank may require collateral, and there may be balance-sheet and FSA solvency issues.

Fixed or floating charges

A charge taken over real property, provided the property is more valuable than the insurer's outstanding entitlement, can be an effective means of mitigating or even eliminating the risk of an intermediary's insolvency. However, assets may not always be available for a fixed charge; and those that are may be subject to prior charges, for example, to banks.

There are other disadvantages:

- a fixed charge over any of its assets means that an intermediary must obtain the chargee's/insurer's consent before dealing in the asset – something it may see as an unacceptable restriction on its business;
- various documentation and other formalities (e.g. registration at Companies House) are required;
- there are balance-sheet and FSA solvency issues;
- floating charges are subordinated to the claims of any fixed charges;
- realising a charge can involve cost and delay.

Separate bank account

A fourth option is for the insurer to stipulate that the intermediary must pay the insurer's funds into a separate bank account, over which the insurer may assert controls: the account could be one opened and operated by the insurer. The downside is that unless the insurer is prepared to accept what could be a heavy administrative burden (particularly where large-scale business is concerned) it will, in reality, want the intermediary to take over a lot of the 'management' of the account – for example, paying claims, making refunds and deducting commission.

The insurer needs to act swiftly to minimise its exposure in the event of a problem. This will mean monitoring the account sufficiently rigorously to be able to identify unusual activity.

Parent company guarantee

A fifth option is a parent company guarantee. This has the advantage of being inexpensive. Its effectiveness, however, depends on the solvency of the parent.

A trust

Finally, an insurer may wish to consider a trust. Trusts come in a variety of forms and in varying degrees of complexity. Where the structure is basic, trust monies should be separated into a designated account immediately or soon after receipt by the intermediary. For a trust to be effective without additional cost and trouble it helps if the trust assets are easily identifiable; this will often not be the case where they are co-mingled with monies held for other insurers or held as part of the intermediary's trading funds.

More complex trust structures can be used – for example, where the intermediary wishes to invest the funds – but these will generally be harder and more expensive to set up and maintain.

A trust will generally work best if the insurer beneficiary takes the trouble to monitor its activities continuously and anticipates any deterioration.

Bank accounts for client money: basic rules

Opening accounts

In setting up client money accounts, the intermediary is required to comply with certain formalities:

1. It must choose an appropriate bank for its clients' money.* It must consider:

■ the bank's capital and deposits and the proportion of them that will be made up of client money;
■ the bank's credit rating;
■ the level of risk in the bank's investment and loan activities.

The intermediary should reassess the bank's suitability at least once a year.

2. It must receive written confirmation from the bank that:

■ the account name distinguishes the account from the intermediary's accounts, for example by including the words 'client' or 'client money' (plus the word 'designated' in the case of designated bank accounts); and
■ all money is held by the intermediary as trustee, and the bank cannot combine the client account(s) with any other or exercise any right of set-off or counterclaim against money held in it/them.

* The rules concerning the choice of bank are set out in CASS 5.5.37G to 5.5.48R.

Managing accounts

Client money accounts must be run according to certain rules. The main ones are summarised below. Where the account is a non-statutory trust, the intermediary must observe additional processes and systems that keep the account in good order – see page 96.

Transference of funds

To a third party

An intermediary may need to transfer client money to a third party; for example, where there is a chain of brokers or other agents. This may only be done if the money is transferred for the purpose of a transaction for the client and, if the client is a retail customer, the client has been notified that their money is being transferred in this way.

Where there is an extended supply chain, each intermediary will owe an obligation to their immediate client to segregate the client money. This means an intermediary cannot sidestep its regulatory obligations by allowing a third party elsewhere in the chain to hold or control client money.

To the client

Client money received by the intermediary must be paid to the client as soon as possible and at least within one business day. This may be by paying it into a client bank account or by paying it to the client directly.

Non-client money

An intermediary can only hold non-client money in a client bank account if:

■ a minimum sum is required to open or keep open the account;
■ interest has been accredited to the intermediary but not yet withdrawn;
■ the object is to protect against temporary shortfalls due to unreconciled items in the account; and

■ the money is part of a mixed remittance and held for a short time.

A firm may pay its own money into a client bank account to ensure client money is protected; however, such funds will become client money and will be subject to the requirements of CASS 5.

Withdrawal of commission

Unless expressly permitted by an agreement between the insurer and insured to do so, intermediaries cannot generally withdraw commission and/or fees from a client's bank account *before* the premium has been paid to the insurers.

Outsourcing

This chapter provides a brief guide to the effective management of outsourcing in the insurance business. It begins with a general introduction to the outsourcing market and its development over recent years. It then looks at some specific uses of outsourcing by insurers and at the mitigation of the legal and practical risks involved.

What is outsourcing?

At its simplest, outsourcing is a commercial arrangement whereby an internally run function is transferred to an external service provider. Arrangements vary according to the nature of the function, but typically involve the transfer of staff, assets and contracts. In turn, the external company provides services to the outsourcing customer on agreed (i.e. contractual) terms.

Outsourcing arrangements extend beyond agency relationships, in which the provider has authority to legally bind the customer (for example, when it supplies a service of intermediation (see Chapter 7)). As the box on page 115 demonstrates, this leads to important differences in the way they are treated by the courts.

What are the current trends?

Outsourcing is not a new concept – businesses have been using contractors for services such as catering, security and property management for decades – but it has evolved significantly over recent years. The principal difference from, say, two or three decades ago is that external providers are now being used for business-critical services – as well as for the more peripheral back-office functions.

The change has, in many ways, been driven by information and communications technology (ICT). Increasingly dependent on IT systems but lacking the skills in-house to manage them, companies have outsourced the IT function to independent specialists.

At the same time, they have taken advantage of advances in technology to transfer elements of customer service, human resources, procurement and finance to providers of 'business process outsourcing' (or BPO) services. Customer enquiries are now often dealt with at remote 'ICT-enabled' call centres; payroll, accounting and procurement processes are automated and handled by someone else.

As the market for outsourcing has grown and matured, the demands of its customers have increased. Clients want to see better returns from contracts. Providers are responding with 'transformational outsourcing' – the promise to launch new initiatives and to re-engineer processes for the strategic good. A BPO specialist may, for example, take over responsibility for the whole of an organisation's indirect procurement spend, centralising and rationalising the buying of non-core items and thereby reducing costs.

Outsourcing today is seen not only as a practical convenience but also as a way of gaining competitive edge. This is reflected in the trend towards offshore outsourcing – whereby companies source services from other countries to take advantage of low labour costs. (The call centres mentioned above are often based overseas.)

How has outsourcing developed in the insurance business?

In the insurance industry, the concept of outsourcing was initially met with caution. Major institutions questioned how external service providers could understand the volume and complexity of their business and the culture of their industry. There were also concerns about the retention of control once services had been outsourced. As in other sectors, outsourcing was limited to the provision of relatively unskilled services that were not seen as lying at the core of the business.

Now, however, the insurance industry is a big contributor to the outsourcing boom. In common with other companies, insurers have recognised the potential of outsourcing to:

■ renew focus on core strategic work through the transfer of 'high-process' activities;
■ reduce IT investment and staff costs; and
■ increase service efficiency and improve customer satisfaction.

Outsourcing in the insurance sector continues to grow rapidly – in terms of both the number of deals and the types of services outsourced. Insurers now frequently outsource services that are important – essential even – to their businesses. And they have been enthusiastic adopters of offshore outsourcing in the drive to control costs.

Some of the main types of business-critical insurance outsourcings are described below. Each of them can be handled from offshore locations offering a round-the-clock, global service.

Call centre outsourcing

Remote call centres are considered to be one of the most successful ways of managing costs. Service providers invest money in infrastructure and state-of-the-art technology to enhance customer 'experience'. In turn, the client avoids IT and staff overheads and makes its customer service more efficient.

Call centre outsourcing arrangements vary in scope and can include both inbound and outbound services. Inbound services will generally cover the management of communication *from* the clients' customers; call centre staff will handle requests for insurance products, queries about existing insurance arrangements and online sales.

Outbound call centre services, as the name suggests, involve call centre agents making calls *to* customers or potential customers on behalf of the client. Outbound services can include telesales and marketing, customer research and surveys and the gathering of market intelligence.

Claims handling outsourcing

Claims handling is key to customer satisfaction and business growth. In recent years, more and more specialist insurance service providers have been coming forward to offer claims handling services. These can include:

■ taking the initial call reporting the claim;

- notifying interested and affected parties, and co-ordinating communications between them;
- managing information relating to the claim;
- tracking the progress of the claim; and
- settling the claim.

Policy administration outsourcing

Policy administration outsourcing varies in scope but services commonly include:

- taking customer calls and collecting and capturing data so that the management of and access to customers' data is prompt and efficient;
- underwriting policies through automated processes that incorporate the client's set underwriting rules and guidelines; and
- dealing with insurance billing and premium payments, handling the printing and mailing of insurance policies, correspondence and product campaigns.

What are the regulatory and legal implications of insurance outsourcing?

FSA requirements

The FSA has developed detailed sets of principles that insurance firms should adopt in any outsourcing arrangements. They outline:

- the factors to be considered before deciding whether to outsource any activities;
- the issues to be covered in the contract with the service provider; and
- the ongoing management of the relationship with the service provider.

Behind them is the general principle that a company does not abdicate responsibility for a service by handing it over to someone else. The overriding obligation of an insurance firm is to take reasonable care to organise and control their affairs responsibly and effectively with adequate risk management systems.

Insurance companies are responsible for ensuring that:

- claims are handled fairly;

■ claims are settled promptly;

■ customers are provided with information on the claims handling procedure, and with an explanation if a claim is rejected, or not settled in full; and

■ insurance intermediaries disclose and manage any conflicts of interest that may exist.

An insurance firm cannot, by outsourcing or delegating its activities to a service provider, avoid any of its legal or regulatory obligations.

Firms are therefore advised by the FSA to put in place 'appropriate safeguards' for any outsourcing or delegation of activities to a service provider. They should:

■ identify, assess and manage the risks arising from an outsourcing arrangement;

■ ensure, both contractually and operationally, that there are appropriate access rights to the service provider's premises, people and information for themselves, their auditors and the regulators;

■ consider contingencies to protect business continuity; and

■ have an exit strategy.

Under FSA regulations, if an insurance firm is intending to enter into, or significantly change, a material outsourcing arrangement it is required to notify the FSA and ensure that the outsourcing does not restrict the FSA in exercising its supervisory powers.

A material outsourcing is one where the services are of such importance that their weakness or failure would cast serious doubt upon the firm's continuing satisfaction of the conditions for FSA authorisation or its compliance with the Principles for Businesses in the FSA Handbook.

Materiality needs to be judged by the firm in relation to the impact of the outsourced service on its activities. The outsourcing of internal audit or compliance and most front-office functions are considered to be material.

A member of the firm's senior management should take responsibility for each material outsourced function. Direct communication lines between this designated person and the individuals responsible for the material outsourced services should be established. The parties should be aware that material outsourcing may be indicative of an agency relationship and may be treated differently in law (see Chapter 7 for further information).

Depending on the nature of the function that is being outsourced, the service provider may itself be carrying on a regulated activity. If that is the case, the service provider should either be authorised by the FSA to carry on that outsourced activity or fall within one of the relevant exemptions (for

example, by being the appointed representative of another authorised firm –
see Chapter 5).

Data protection requirements

The insurance outsourcings described above have obvious implications for
data protection. They will inevitably involve the transfer of information
about customers and their policies – much of it personal and/or sensitive in
nature. (In some cases, details of medical records will need to be passed on.)

The UK Data Protection Act 1998 (DPA) requires the contract between
the outsourcing client and the service provider to impose certain data
security requirements.

When the outsourcing arrangement is with another UK company, or one
based elsewhere in Europe, compliance is usually relatively easy: both
parties will be subject to the same rules. The situation gets more complex
when the service provider is based outside the EEA. Under the Data
Protection Directive of 1995, implemented in the UK by the DPA, European
firms are restricted in terms of the data that can be transferred or stored
outside the EEA without equivalent rules and enforcement. The principle is
that policyholders should be guaranteed the level of protection they would
have inside the EEA. Some countries have been deemed to be 'safe' by the
European Commission, for example, Canada and Argentina.

Where the outsourcing client enters into an outsourcing arrangement with
a service provider to process personal information on its behalf, it remains
liable for the security of the data and is deemed to retain control over it. In
other words, the insurance company remains liable for any breaches of the
DPA, even if the service provider is based abroad.

When sourcing services from others, the insurance company, as the data
controller, must either: obtain the consent of each individual data subject; or
put in place sufficient protections for the rights of the data subjects.

The former would be an impractical and expensive option for a large
insurance company to undertake for all of its existing customers (although it
could be built into the process of signing up new customers). The practical
alternative is for the insurance company to enter into a contract that requires
the data processor (i.e. the relevant service provider) to respect the same
data protection obligations that the company is under. The European
Commission has issued a set of model contract clauses that should be used
for this purpose.

Failure to comply with the data protection requirements may result in
enforcement action by the Information Commissioner and compensation
claims from individuals. There is also the risk of damage from bad publicity.

How should outsourcing contracts be drawn up?

The framework

The contractual framework for an outsourcing will typically take the form of a transfer agreement and a services agreement. Where the outsourcing involves the transfer of staff, assets and contracts the transfer agreement will govern and regulate the terms on which this happens.

In many cases, the outsourcing will be subject to TUPE – The Transfer of Undertakings (Protection of Employment) Regulations, which were updated and extended in 2006. Part I of Chapter 13 explains in detail the circumstances where this will happen.

If TUPE does apply, the staff of the outsourcing client who are engaged in the services to be transferred will become employees of the service provider. The liabilities relating to the affected staff (for example, in relation to pensions) will also transfer to the service provider. This means that the transfer agreement will need to include indemnities relating to the employees pre and post transfer so that risk and liability is fairly apportioned between the parties (see Chapter 13, Part I, for further details.)

The transfer agreement will also apportion risk and liability for past and future events relating to the assets and contracts which fall within the scope of the outsourcing.

The transfer element of an outsourcing is usually separate from the services agreement because it is treated as a one-time transaction that enables the parties to ring-fence the liabilities associated with the transfer. The services agreement, on the other hand, defines the ongoing relationship between the client and service provider. It will govern and regulate the arrangement, and its terms will cover:

- the scope of the services to be provided;
- the service levels and standards of performance expected from the service provider;
- the charges payable by the client;
- the way the relationship between the client and the service provider will be managed; and
- the exit and termination arrangements.

Understanding the service scope

Both the client and the service provider must have a clear understanding of the precise scope of the outsourced services. Otherwise the arrangement is likely to fail. Poor definition of what the provider will and will not do can have potentially serious consequences for the client, including: a service that does not meet expectations and requirements; and additional costs (the service provider will bill separately for services that it sees as falling outside the contracted scope).

Defining the scope will mean defining 'boundaries'. The client must decide how the outsourced services will interface with those functions it retains itself or outsources to other providers. Where the client is considering multi-supplier or selective outsourcing it should also think about who should take primary responsibility for the associated risks. Who will be best placed to resolve any problems: the client or one of the service providers? Who will be best able to *manage* the interfaces?

Managing service performance

The services agreement should specify the levels of service performance that the client needs to run its business. The service levels must be realistic and affordable. And they must be capable of measurement – otherwise it will be impossible to monitor the service provider's performance and form an objective assessment of whether the outsourcing is delivering benefits.

As part of the decision to outsource, the client will be seeking better services for the same or a lower price than could be provided in-house and also new improved processes and services.

The drive for continuous improvement should be clear to the service provider. It's important, however, for the client to set priorities: the service provider will need to be able to distinguish the key service levels from those that are more marginal. And it's important also to get the number of levels right: too many, and the provider will feel stifled or unable to do its job; too few, and the service delivery incentive may be lost.

Responsibility for monitoring and reporting on service performance is usually placed with the service provider, but the client should hold regular service review meetings and have the right to verify and audit the service provider's service reports. It will need to know the methodology is robust. In a call centre outsourcing, for example, it should ask how the performance of workers is assessed. Are 'customer service advisers' polite to people and do they work effectively and efficiently? How is the customer's experience assessed? Are calls recorded etc?

Consequences of poor service performance

It is normal to impose sanctions on the service provider for deficient performance. A regime involving the payment of service credits and liquidated damages is common.

Service credits and liquidated damages are both forms of payment (or credit) that the parties agree in advance as compensation for deficient service provision. Although the terms tend to be used interchangeably, there are significant differences between them, and these are explained below.

Service credits generally involve payments of smaller sums of money. They are usually recovered as a deduction from the service charges, claimed because the client has not received the services it contracted for.

Liquidated damages, in contrast, generally involve more substantial sums of money and are recovered in respect of service failures that have the potential to cause the client to suffer financial losses. They are calculated by reference to the outsourcing client's estimated potential loss. There are complex legal rules surrounding the calculation of liquidated damages, and outsourcing customers need to take care not to infringe them.

Service credits and liquidated damages are generally negotiated and debated as part of discussions on pricing, indemnities and limitations of liability. The service provider will invariably price the services to reflect the amount of risk it is taking on – the payment of service credits and liquidated damages and its own level of liability will all be factored in.

Governance

The governance structure in an outsourcing forms the foundation on which the customer and the service provider will manage and develop the overall relationship and monitor the provision of the outsourced services. It defines the organisational relationships, communication mechanisms and decision-making processes to ensure the success of the outsourcing arrangement. Where the structure is weak, so too is the outsourcing.

The governance structure proposed tends to mirror the business structure of the client, who will often require representation from internal functions such as tax and finance, audit and compliance and operations, and internal users of the services. The service provider can be required to have a team that matches or works alongside the client's internal management levels.

One key purpose of the governance structure is to provide a process for resolving problems at the appropriate level of seniority. However, it is important to ensure that the levels of representation are not so complex or cumbersome as to restrict or delay the decision-making process.

A comprehensive governance process allows for some degree of contractual flexibility: it's a mechanism for discussing, approving and incorporating service innovations. For it to work, the client must retain a skilled in-house team with the authority to manage the outsourcing arrangement with its service provider. This fact is sometimes overlooked by the client when outsourcing – to the detriment of the arrangement.

While the ultimate power to resolve issues in an outsourcing arrangement usually rests with the client, the service provider needs effective representation so that issues can be resolved jointly. The governance structure must not degenerate into a forum for chiding the provider for weaknesses in the service or for using the provider as a scapegoat.

Incorporating a governance structure in which all parties are included and heard can minimise the risks of legal disputes. It results in a stronger relationship between the parties – for their mutual benefit.

Exit management

A successful outsourcing client thinks about what will happen *after* the term of the contract as well as during it. The ability to ensure a smooth exit or transition on expiry or termination is as important as managing the agreement *during* the term.

Outsourced services are usually key business services that the client requires in order to provide services to its own customers and/or run its own business. Therefore, any period of disjointed or disrupted service between providers will be unacceptable.

Whether it is taking a service back in-house or transferring it to another external provider, a company will need the security of continuous service provision. This is more likely to be achieved if expectations are clear regarding the client's requirements for exit and the costs of the provision of exit activities are understood.

In negotiating an outsourcing agreement, clients sometimes ignore exit provisions on the basis that they can be dealt with during the term. This is a mistake. If an outsourcing fails, the relationship between client and service provider is likely to break down, making the agreement of a comprehensive exit plan almost impossible. The time to consider how best to transition the services *from* the provider is when you're considering how best to transition services *to* the provider. Like everything else in the contract, exit provisions must be clear.

Addressing regulatory requirements

The client should ensure that the services supplied under the arrangement meet both legal and regulatory requirements. Essentially, the services agreement must do three things:

i)   impose compliance obligations on the service provider;
ii) preclude any rights or obligations that would fetter in any way the rights of any regulator – e.g. the FSA; and
iii) give rights to the client that enable it to meet FSA requirements and guidelines.

More specifically, the client must be able to:

■ undertake appropriate audits and reviews (whether held by internal auditors or external auditors such as the FSA);
■ take control of the provision of the services in circumstances where the service provider is failing (commonly known as the right of 'step-in');
■ terminate the outsourcing arrangement – for example, in circumstances where there has been a change of control of the service provider or where the service provider is in material default of its contractual obligations;
■ require the service provider to implement the detailed exit plan to ensure an orderly transfer of the services back to the outsourcing client or to a replacement service provider;
■ require the service provider to comply with robust and stringent security requirements to prevent security breaches; and
■ require the service provider to plan and implement disaster recovery arrangements.

Remember that compliance is ultimately the responsibility of the outsourcing client. The above, therefore, represents a system of risk control. The insurer must limit its own liabilities by actively managing its relationship with the service provider – the first step being a watertight services agreement.

VAT consequences of outsourcing

Insurance-related services provided by insurance brokers and agents are VAT exempt. Does the same exemption apply to insurance-related services that are outsourced? A recent case suggests not.

On 3 March 2005 the European Court of Justice (ECJ) issued its decision in the Arthur Andersen/Accenture VAT case. Accenture had been contracted by Universal Life, the insurance company, to carry out services such as accepting and checking insurance applications, handling insurance policy changes and managing claims. The ECJ ruled that these services did not fall within the VAT exemption because Accenture did not qualify as an insurance agent or broker.

The potential consequence of the ruling is that where back-office insurance-related functions are outsourced, the service provider will charge the insurance company 17.5 per cent VAT on its fee. In other words, the costs of outsourcing insurance services could increase: the supply of insurance is VAT exempt within the EU so the insurer wouldn't be able to claim the additional money back.

HMRC considered UK legislation in light of the ECJ judgement and concluded that the current exemption for insurance-related services was drawn too widely and would need to be amended. HMRC interpreted the ECJ judgment to mean that in order to qualify for VAT exemption as an insurance agent or broker the service provider would need to be carrying out a service of independent intermediation – i.e. finding prospective customers, introducing them to an insurer and then negotiating a policy it had no material interest in.

As of early 2007, the UK government is monitoring developments within the EU before deciding how and when to implement any legislative changes. Its decision could see insurance companies reassessing the commercial proposition of their outsourcing arrangements.

Use of technology

Insurance companies increasingly rely on technology in the course of their business when dealing with both customers and third parties. This chapter looks at the legal and practical implications. It concentrates on two areas: online selling and servicing and the use of personal data.

I   Selling and servicing online

What's the legal framework?

Many of the laws affecting financial services providers apply whether the transaction takes places on- or offline. At the same time, there is a growing body of UK legislation dealing with e-commerce and, in particular, the provision of financial services over the internet. Much of this legislation originates in EU directives.

One of the aims is to make sure that there's a level playing field – that a customer's *rights* aren't affected by buying online. This is mainly achieved by the directives and regulations listed below.

E-commerce directive

The Electronic Commerce (EC Directive) Regulations 2002 require that anyone providing online services makes certain information directly and permanently accessible to consumers. Such information includes the provider's name, postal address, company registered number and VAT number. Relevant Directive provisions have been incorporated into ICOB 4 (see Chapter 4).

The requirement applies to websites (whether used for sales or infor-mation purposes) and to commercial communications made by e-mail or text message.

All prices must be clear and unambiguous, and state whether they are inclusive of taxes and delivery costs, and certain contractual information must be supplied.

The most common way of fulfilling these requirements is to include the required information in the terms and conditions of sale and ensure that consumers are clearly and explicitly directed to read them.

The service provider must then set out its terms and conditions of sale in a way that allows users to save and print them.

Electronic signatures directive

The Electronic Communications Act 2000 and the Electronic Signatures Regulations 2002 deal with the legal recognition of electronic signatures and the process whereby they are verified, generated or communicated, and the removal of obstacles in other legislation to the use of electronic commu-nication and storage in place of paper.

Many insurance products had largely relied on traditional 'wet' (i.e. ink on paper) signatures. In the online environment various electronic signa-tures can be used. At the simplest level, an electronic signature could be a user clicking the 'buy' button on a website. Electronic signatures could also take the form of scanned manuscript signatures, typed signatures or digital signatures.

Directive on distance marketing of financial services

The Financial Services (Distance Marketing) Regulations 2004 set out the information that must be supplied to consumers before concluding a contract 'at a distance'. They govern the sale of pensions, mortgages and other financial services products to consumers by the internet, e-mail, telephone, fax or post – i.e. any 'remote' means. The provisions of the Directive are incorporated into ICOB 4 (see Chapter 4) but also apply when ICOB doesn't.

The consumer must receive specific information in relation to the product provider's identity, the product and the contract particulars both before and after the contract is concluded. This information, together with the contractual terms and conditions, must be provided in a clear and compre-hensible manner on paper or another durable medium (which includes e-mail).

The consumer must be given the opportunity to withdraw from the concluded contract without incurring liability during a specified cancel-lation period (often referred to as a 'cooling-off' period). The cancellation period begins only when the copy of the contract terms and conditions is received by the customer. If specified conditions are fulfilled, this period is 14 days (30 days for life insurance or personal pension contracts).

The contract is terminated from the date notice of cancellation is given, and the provider must give a refund within 30 days of that date.

Privacy and Electronic Communications Regulations 2003

These Regulations affect all organisations that market by telephone, fax, automated calling systems, e-mail, short message service (SMS) and multimedia message service (MMS) – or any other form of electronic communication – and apply alongside the Data Protection Act 1998.

The prior consent of individuals is generally required before sending out e-mail marketing messages, and an organisation needs to determine how best to obtain this consent.

The Regulations require information to be made available about the use of 'cookies', which store information about customers' activities on websites, and marketers must not conceal or disguise the identity of the sender or the party on whose behalf the marketing is done.

The Disability Discrimination Act 1995

The Disability Discrimination Act 1995 means that a company must make available to the disabled services it provides to the public at large. The Act includes 'access to and use of information services' among its examples of services to which the provisions apply.

Reasonable steps must be taken to make websites accessible to the disabled. If your site does not meet certain design standards, you could (in theory at least) be sued for discrimination.

A website should comply with a minimum accessibility level defined by the standards-setting body, the World Wide Web Consortium, or W3C. The prescribed levels are A, AA and AAA, and it is advisable to aim for AA compliance as a minimum.

Accessibility standards should be addressed in the contract with the website developer. A simple website check can be carried out using one of the accessibility tools freely available on the internet. Any problems that are identified should then be solved.

How can insurers manage the risks of e-commerce?

Online sales of insurance products – made directly to consumers or via third-party 'distribution channels' – are increasing. The industry preferred approach is straight-through online processing, where the application is completed and submitted online without the need for signed documentation or product provider intervention.

While this approach saves time and money, it carries risks. It is important to remember, though, that many of the hazards of online selling and servicing apply offline, too. The potential for fraud, for example, is essentially no greater than it is in paper-based applications.

While risk cannot be eliminated entirely, it can be reduced to an acceptable level through the relevant contracts – with the customer and third-party service providers – and through careful attention to and control of the online sales process.

Contracts with customers

The formalities for contracting online and offline are essentially the same, but it is important to get the online sales process right to ensure that the contract is properly formed and enforceable.

As mentioned earlier, the product terms and conditions must be brought to the customer's attention to ensure their proper incorporation into the contract. The customer must be given the chance to review and indicate acceptance of the terms before conclusion of the contract. Offline acceptance of the terms is indicated by signing the application form; online acceptance may be indicated by checking a box or clicking a button.

The provider must be able to show what terms the customer has accepted. It is essential that it retains a permanent record of the concluded contract, together with the information the customer was given at the time. The Financial Ombudsman Service has indicated that this record need not be a signed application form. However, the provider must be able to demonstrate the integrity of whatever record it has retained; having a secure audit trail is key.

Selling through third parties

When selling directly to a customer, the product provider maintains control of what is presented to an applicant on the screen and when. Where a third party is involved there is a greater risk of non-disclosure of material facts, and of the customer's attention not being drawn to the policy terms. A provider may have difficulties relying on contractual exclusion clauses if the sales process was inadequate.

Popular online distribution channels include intermediary extranets, portals, content aggregators and 'white-labelled' sites such as those run by supermarkets and other corporate partners (see Chapter 5).

While each of these models presents different issues, there will be common themes in contracts:

■ **Data.** Who is responsible for collecting customer data? What if the wrong data is collected? What if data is corrupted or modified during transmission?

■ **Intellectual property rights.** What rights does each party have to use the data and branding and web content of the other? Are these rights restricted to online activities? How will competitors' brands be displayed together (e.g. on content aggregator sites)?

■ **System and sales process.** Who is responsible for the marketing and selling activities? Who will verify and authenticate users (see below)? Whose terms and conditions will be presented to the user? Will the sales process be specified by the product provider or dictated by the third-party service provider? Are minimum security and system standards in place to ensure secure storage and transmission of data?

■ **Compliance.** Who is responsible for ensuring that the website and sales process comply with FSA regulations and the law?

The contract between the insurance company and the service provider must clearly define the parties' respective roles and responsibilities.

Online servicing

In addition to selling insurance products online, companies often provide online facilities for servicing policies – e.g. for tracking the progress of customer applications. While these facilities might be offered to customers directly, they are more commonly provided first to intermediaries on provider extranets or through portal sites.

Use of a portal site involves the introduction of a trusted third party to the relationship between the product provider and the intermediary. In most cases, the third party will be responsible for authenticating the parties (i.e. the product provider and intermediary) and transferring data between them.

Careful consideration must be given to the contractual arrangements with the third party, to protect both the provider and intermediary. Online servicing will involve the use of personal data on customers and confidential data on policies and therefore has data protection implications (see section II, below).

Many providers insist on the use of Origo Standards for the transfer of electronic data to and from intermediaries. These are industry technical standards, developed by the UK life assurance and pensions industry body Origo Services Limited, which are used to securely transfer data between an intermediary and a product provider directly or via a trusted third party. For certain provider services (including tracking, commission and contract enquiry) the provider and intermediary can choose to adopt Origo's standard legal framework – this addresses the security and contractual issues surrounding electronic transfer of data between them, both directly and via the trusted third party.

Proving the identity of users

There are several regulatory reasons why it is essential to verify someone's identity. These include preventing the sale of inappropriate goods to minors and ensuring the consumer is based in a country where the product provider is authorised.

There are commercial reasons, too. Establishing identity will:

■ ensure the party has capacity to contract;
■ prevent the party later claiming that they are not bound by the contract; and
■ assist in tackling fraud.

Once a contract has been entered into, identity will need to be authenticated each time the service is used.

In the 'real' or 'bricks and mortar' world, verification and authentication are (in theory at least) relatively easy. On opening a new bank account, your identity is *verified* when you appear in person at the bank and present your passport and a utility bill. Your identity is *authenticated* by use of a pin number at an automated teller machine (ATM). Online, alternative methods must be sought.

Establishing identity

To be satisfied that the person you are dealing with exists and they are who they say they are, you may need to verify the person's information against evidence from another source, such as a credit reference agency. If the provider chooses to carry out identity checks online (e.g. by using commercially available solutions such as Experian) it must have a process for retaining the evidence gathered.

The process of verification should be sufficiently rigorous for the products and services being sold. It should reflect the risks involved – not least the damage that could be caused by misuse of identity.

Authentication of identity

The means of authentication could be:

■ something that the person knows such as a password;
■ something the person possesses such as a digital certificate or key fob;
■ something that is a physical feature unique to the person such as a fingerprint or retinal scan.

The more sophisticated the means, the greater the degree of certainty but the higher the cost. It is important that a business carefully considers the degree of certainty actually required and selects a method of authentication right for the nature of the products and services being supplied online.

In reaching its decision, it will need to consider: the data protection implications of the particular method; and the accessibility of the method; is it user-friendly?

Username and password is the most common form of authentication for selling and servicing products online. However, it is not the most secure. A complex password using different characters is more difficult to crack, but there is no guarantee that a user will keep their password 'safe'.

In the financial services industry, digital certificates are increasingly used as an alternative to usernames and passwords. Sometimes described as electronic 'passports', these use cryptography to give users a unique identity. Importantly, they can improve security by removing the need for multiple usernames and passwords. For example, Unipass digital certificates, offered by Origo Secure Internet Services (OSIS), give intermediaries access across provider extranets and portals.

Checklist: compliance with e-commerce laws

Fulfilling the detailed requirements of e-commerce legislation means asking:

- Are consumers being provided with the required information?
- Do the terms and conditions of sale comply with e-commerce and financial services legislation?
- Does the sales process comply with e-commerce legislation?
- Have the appropriate consents been obtained for e-marketing?
- Is the website accessible and useable?

II   Use of personal data

What are the rules for collection and processing of personal data?

Insurers and their intermediaries habitually collect, process, store and transfer information on customers and policies. In doing so, they must, as stated in the previous chapter, comply with the DPA. Failure to follow the rules can mean enforcement action by the Information Commissioner, criminal liability and loss of reputation. This, together with the fact that UK auditors are increasingly reporting on a company's internal controls, puts pressure on organisations to put protection of data high on their list of priorities.

The DPA requires anyone processing personal data to do so in accordance with eight common-sense data protection principles. Some of the key ones are discussed below.

Fair and lawful processing

The first data protection principle requires personal data to be collected and used fairly and lawfully. Data subjects are able to seek compensation for improper use of their personal data.

Fair and lawful use is that it corresponds to the specific purposes for which the data was collected. An organisation must be clear about why it wishes to process personal data and about whether its purposes are fair and lawful. If it is not, it should not begin the process of data collection.

People who are data subjects should be notified of the fact and provided with certain information in a 'fair collection notice' or 'data protection notice'. 'Certain information' includes:

- the identity of the organisation (the data controller);
- the purposes for processing; and
- anything else that is needed to be fair to the subject – such as how long the information will be kept and whether the controller plans to process personal data outside the EEA.

In addition, data controllers need to be able to point to one of the specified grounds in Schedule 2 of the DPA for processing personal data, and if processing sensitive personal data, a further ground under Schedule 3. One of the grounds for processing is consent, and organisations will therefore need to think about how consent can best be built into online processes and terms and conditions. (For sensitive data the consent needs to be *explicit.*)

Security

The seventh principle of the DPA creates obligations of security. The data controller is required to take appropriate technical and organisational measures to protect the personal data that it holds from loss or corruption or 'attack'. The former include firewalls and anti-virus software. The latter include disaster recovery planning, staff training and user and customer education.

The security systems should provide adequate protection and should reflect current technological developments. (The definition of adequate will, however, vary from company to company and it may not be necessary to have the most sophisticated and expensive solutions available.)

If personal data is to be processed by a third party (a 'data processor'), the contractual arrangements must make security obligations clear; essentially, the data processor must be required to comply with obligations equivalent to those imposed on the data controller by the seventh principle of the DPA.

Ultimately, responsibility rests with the data controller. As part of its risk management, therefore, it should choose a processor carefully and take reasonable steps to ensure its compliance with security measures. The first of these is a contract made or evidenced in writing under which the third party agrees to process the data only on the instructions of the controller and provides certain security guarantees.

As well as thinking about the ability of staff and contractors to fulfil security requirements, an organisation must think about its customers and their 'education'. Do they know about practices such as 'phishing' and 'pharming' and what suspicious signals to look out for? Do they know how to report suspected attacks? Both 'phishing' and 'pharming' pose serious security threats. The former involves the sending of e-mails claiming to be from legitimate financial organisations to recipients, who are then redirected to a fraudulent website. Once there, they are invited to update personal information that is then used for fraudulent purposes such as identity theft. 'Pharming' is an attack that aims to redirect one website's traffic to another (bogus) website and then misuse the details entered on that site.

Other issues

The DPA is not the only law that applies to the processing of personal data. A company may be liable under other laws, too.

If, for example, an insurer makes an unauthorised disclosure of information sourced from medical records or of other confidential data it may be sued by the customer for damages. (In other words, it may be held to have breached its duty of confidence to the client.) Where marketing is involved, there may be a breach of the Privacy and Electronic Communications Regulations 2003.

The American Sarbanes–Oxley Act (SOX), the UK Companies (Audit, Investigations and Community Enterprise) Act 2004 and Basel II (European banking legislation) may also influence the information security policies of financial services providers.

What are the rules for data sharing?

Commercially, data sharing makes good business sense: customer data is increasingly seen as a valuable asset. There is nothing in the DPA that says you cannot share personal data. The DPA simply provides a framework within which sharing should take place.

Thinking about what you tell customers in data protection notices and if and how you will seek consent will go a long way to allowing you to use your customer data for what you want to use it for. Remember, though, not to overlook other issues such as confidentiality and intellectual property ownership.

This section pulls together some of the issues mentioned previously, and considers the more common scenarios in which data may be shared.

In each scenario, the importance of setting out clearly at the outset what you will be doing with the data cannot be overemphasised. Get this first stage wrong and you could be prevented from using the customer data in the way you want; there could be costly re-collection exercises and even involvement by the Information Commissioner. Get it right and you will be able to use a valuable business asset to maximum advantage.

What are the common data-sharing scenarios?

Intra-group data sharing

Data may be shared within the corporate group for marketing, fraud prevention, research and customer profiling or corporate reorganisation reasons. In order to comply with the first data protection principle, the following will be important considerations:

■ What has the company collecting the personal data told the customer about what will happen to it?
■ Did the data protection notice provide that the data would only be processed for a very specific purpose; or was it drafted widely enough to cover processing for purposes such as marketing etc?
■ Were customers told that their data would be shared with group companies? Are group companies based outside the EEA – and in countries that the EU has not deemed 'safe' for data protection purposes? (See Chapter 10.)

Data sharing with introducers

It is increasingly common for insurers to want to share information with a corporate partner; for example, a supermarket that decides to enter the world of selling financial services online. This scenario raises a number of issues, including:

- Who wants to market to the customer and what do they want to be able to market?
- Is the customer aware that marketing may not be limited to the specific insurance sold but may extend to the whole range of products and services typically offered by a financial services company, as well as the whole range of products and services provided by the supermarket?

The parties and their group companies may want to use the customer data collected to detect and prevent fraud and to build up a more comprehensive profile of the customer. The supermarket (or other corporate partner) should ensure that its privacy policy and terms and conditions make *all* the uses that will be made of the data by *all* the companies involved absolutely clear. It will not be sufficient to refer only to fraud prevention and marketing if customer profiles will be generated, customer data will be aggregated and confidential medical or financial information will be shared.

Each company involved may wish to consider separately what rights it has to use the customer data. The following questions will be key:

- Does the supermarket place any restrictions on the other companies and might it wish to do so?
- Who owns the database in which the customer data sits?
- Who has access to this database and what rights do they have?

Sharing within the financial services sector

There may be circumstances where product providers will want to share data with competitors; for example, for the purposes of fraud avoidance or detection or credit referencing. There are various industry bodies that exist for these purposes, including CIFAS (Credit Industry Fraud Avoidance Scheme) and the credit reference agencies.

Increasingly, providers are forming partnerships – for example, where a home contents insurance provider offers another underwriter's car insurance cover to its customers.

Such partnerships can provide considerable commercial benefits – not least, greater exposure to consumers, expansion into new areas and positive 'marketing imagery' (brand associations etc). There must, however, be specific guidelines in the partnership agreement about how data sharing should be managed.

Checklist: data sharing

As pages 125 and 126 have made clear, an insurance company may need to share information with group companies, regulatory bodies such as the FSA or competitors. In each of these scenarios, a number of issues will need to be contractually addressed. The main ones are listed below:

- Who will do what?
- Who is responsible both legally and commercially for providing the data protection notice to customers and for the security of the data?
- Who has the relationship with the customer?
- Whose website is collecting customers' personal data? Whose branding is being used to market the services to customers? Is it clear to the customer who is involved?
- Who owns the customer data?
- Who is the data controller under the DPA? (There may be more than one data controller for any one set of personal data.)
- Who owns the intellectual property rights in the data? For example, who owns any copyright and database rights?
- What other products can be marketed to the customer?
- What has the customer been told will happen to their personal data in the data protection notice? Does this cover marketing by the insurance company/group companies/third parties?
- How is the data to be shared?
- With whom will parties share the data (e.g. group companies, competitors, regulatory bodies, intermediaries)? What are customers told about this in the data protection notice?

The key contractual themes include:

- **Compliance.** Under the DPA, who are the legal data controllers with compliance obligations? Are there any data processors acting on behalf of the data controllers? How is compliance ensured?
- **IPR ownership.** The data controller of data in a database is not automatically the owner of the intellectual property rights in the data or the database. If the data has been collected by a third party, ownership may rest with that third party; any use of the data may be subject to licensing conditions.
- **Confidentiality.** Does the customer expect that certain types of information will not be disclosed to others, e.g. medical information? Are they right to expect this? Is all customer data confidential? How does confidentiality affect a company's ability to exploit its customer lists commercially?

■ **Customer terms and conditions.** Are these consistent with what has been agreed commercially? Can they be amended if necessary? Are there processes to track which customers are subject to which version of the terms?

Online brands: key issues

The intellectual property rights in a brand are often one of the most valuable assets of a business. This is reflected in the growth of 'white labelling', whereby one party sells its products under the well-known and well-respected 'name' of another.

A business must protect its rights in its brand both on- and offline, and enforce them to prevent another business 'piggybacking' on its reputation. However, it is equally important to avoid infringing the rights of another party.

The 'brand' may consist of several elements – a name, logo, product design, slogan, jingle – and be protected by different intellectual property rights. Here, we will focus on trademarks and domain names, which are most relevant to online brands.

Trademarks

A trademark distinguishes the goods or services offered by one business from those of another, and can be a name, words, logos, pictures, tag lines – even sounds and smells. In the UK, a trademark can be protected under the common law tort of 'passing off' and by registration with the UK Trade Marks Registry. (Infringement of a registered trademark is much cheaper and easier to prove than infringement of an unregistered mark.)

Companies should consider:

■ what they want to register as their mark;
■ whether somebody else has already registered the chosen brand name;
■ whether the trademark is capable of being registered. (The mark must be distinctive and not descriptive.)

Registration is country-specific: a trademark registered in the UK will only be given protection in the UK. A business should look at all of the countries in which it intends to trade online and consider registering the brand in each.

Once registered, the brand should be controlled across the business; only consistent use will build the brand in the mind of consumers. The business should also monitor what competitors and potential competitors are doing to ensure its IPR rights are not being infringed.

Domain names

Domain names are unique names that identify internet sites. They usually consist of two parts: the name of the business or the brand associated with the business and the suffix such as .co.uk or .com. No statutory protection is afforded to domain names. They are not intellectual property rights under UK law, and there is no action for 'domain name infringement' as such. However, the UK courts have been willing to use the laws of 'passing off' and trademarks to tackle domain name infringement.

Given the importance and value of a domain name to a business, there can often be a race to be first to 'claim' a name, and this can lead to disputes on the 'right' to register. Cybersquatting (registering a domain name in bad faith) and typosquatting (registering domain names that are nearly identical to the actual domain names used by other businesses) are common causes of contention.

Domain-name cases are usually heard by a dispute resolution panel, such as the World Intellectual Property Organisation (WIPO), but some businesses have opted to take the cybersquatters and typosquatters to court and have had claims for passing off and trademark infringement upheld.

When choosing and protecting a domain name, the following will be important questions:

■ Is our brand part of our domain name? Have we registered our brand as a trademark?
■ Has someone registered similar names? (If so there is the possibility of infringement – either by you or by another party in your mark.)

To give yourself maximum protection, you should register:

■ as many top-level domains as possible (e.g. .com .net .org);
■ domains for each country where you plan to trade; and
■ common misspellings in order to prevent typosquatters.

This, though, has cost implications.

Once you have registered your domain names, you should monitor and check regularly whether any similar domains have been registered, and make someone responsible for renewing the domain-name registrations. Failure to renew will mean that your rights to the domain name lapse.

12

Insurance and competition law

Open and healthy competition is good for both consumers and businesses. It means more choice and better value for consumers and it creates a level playing field on which all companies have the chance to flourish. These are the principles on which competition law is based. Companies in the insurance sector need to be aware of competition law not only so they can meet their obligations under it and avoid the risks of infringement but also so they can assert their rights and protect their positions in the marketplace.

What are the rules?

Anti-competitive agreements and conduct that may affect trade within the UK are prohibited by Chapters I and II of the Competition Act 1998. Where the effect of the anti-competitive arrangements or behaviour may be felt across EU member states, they are prohibited by Articles 81 and 82 of the EC Treaty.

UK and EU competition law prohibit two main types of anti-competitive activity: anti-competitive agreements between businesses; and abuse of a dominant market position.

Underwriters and intermediaries that compete within the insurance or reinsurance market must avoid any agreements, however informal, that have the object or effect of restricting competition between them. They must always avoid any collusive arrangements in relation to the premiums they charge and the specific terms and conditions offered to their customers.

Insurance undertakings with a dominant position in a particular product or geographic market must also avoid any conduct that could be considered to abuse that market power to the detriment of competitors or customers. These rules apply whether an arrangement to distribute insurance is between underwriters and their agents, distributors, brokers or intermediaries or between competing underwriters – in other words, whether it is vertical or horizontal.

Do the rules apply to all agreements?

To be caught by the prohibition on anti-competitive agreements, there must be an agreement between businesses, decisions by associations of businesses or concerted practices that prevent, restrict or distort competition in the EU or UK to an appreciable extent or are intended to do so and that may affect trade in the EU or UK.

Agreements between companies in the same corporate group are generally not caught by the competition rules as they are not regarded as separate economic entities. Similarly, an agreement between a company and a 'genuine' agent generally falls outside the scope of the rules as such an agent is regarded as part of the same economic entity as its principal. An intermediary is likely to be a 'genuine' agent under a pure introducer arrangement – that is, if it undertakes limited risk in relation to the contracts it introduces or concludes on behalf of an underwriter and is not contractually bound either to undertake market-specific sunk investment (i.e. a cost incurred on entering a market that is not recoverable on exiting that market, for example, investments in branding, distribution and production technology) or to meet significant ongoing costs that are not reimbursed by the underwriter.

What constitutes an agreement?

Whether an agreement is anti-competitive is assessed on the basis of its effect on competition or its objective, rather than its wording or form. This means that verbal, written, informal and formal agreements are all capable of being anti-competitive (e.g. a 'gentleman's agreement' or a deal done over the telephone). Moreover, conduct by two or more parties that falls short of an agreement or decision but arises from some form of direct or indirect contact or co-operation between competitors (however informal) may be treated as a concerted practice. Decisions or recommendations by associations of undertakings, such as trade associations, can also be caught by the prohibition on anti-competitive agreements.

What constitutes an 'appreciable effect'?

Whether an agreement has an appreciable effect on competition can depend, amongst other things, on the market shares of the parties to the agreement, the content of the agreement and the market in which the parties operate.

In determining whether there has been an unlawful restriction of competition, the competition authorities will carry out an analysis of the relevant product and geographic markets. Once these have been identified, the parties' relative commercial positions in the identified markets will be assessed, in particular their market shares. In general, market shares of less than 10 per cent (for agreements between competitors) or 15 per cent (for vertical agreements) in the relevant market will usually mean that the competition rules do not apply as they will not be considered to have an appreciable effect on competition.

However, 'hard core' restrictions of competition will be caught by the rules regardless of the market shares involved. The authorities take the view that certain types of agreement, by their very nature, always restrict competition to an appreciable extent and so are prohibited under competition law. These include:

■ agreements that have, as their object or effect, direct or indirect price fixing or resale price maintenance, the limit or control of production, markets, technical development or investment, and market or customer sharing;
■ binding or non-binding recommendations about rates, premiums, charges and discounts; and
■ agreements not to offer rebates or discounts.

The general rule is that anti-competitive agreements are prohibited unless they are excluded or exempted from the competition rules. In the insurance/reinsurance sector, a distinction can be drawn between agreements setting general risk premiums, which may be lawful, and those setting specific commercial premiums, which are always likely to infringe the competition rules. This is because the risk premium is considered to be an amount that can be objectively determined according to the net cost of the cover (i.e. the size of the insured risk and the frequency with which this risk occurs). By contrast, the commercial premium should only be determined by the individual insurers or reinsurers concerned as it corresponds to the risk premium plus the administrative costs and the profit margin of the individual insurers or reinsurers.

How are markets defined?

As the above suggests, much hinges on the parties' positions in the relevant product markets. In insurance and reinsurance, product markets are generally defined narrowly.

Underwriting and brokerage of insurance have been defined as separate markets by the Office of Fair Trading (OFT) and European Commission (EC) (*KKR/Willis Corroon* (1998), *Marsh McLennan/Sedgwick* (1998), *QBE International Holdings/MBP Holdings* (2005)). Those cases established that insurers market their own products and have a vested commercial interest in selling them to their clients, whereas brokers act as intermediaries between (re)insurers and clients, acting on their clients' behalf and seeking to place their clients' risk with the most suitable and competitive insurers.

The EC has also identified separate markets for life insurance and reinsurance products on the basis that there are different levels of risk associated with each (*UAP/Transatlantic/Sun Life* (1991)). If different products have different risks then each product will be considered a separate market for the purpose of establishing the relevant product market.

In general, the EC distinguishes three market segments when assessing cases in the insurance sector: general insurance, life insurance (subdivided into life assurance policies, investment policies and pensions) and reinsurance (*CGU/Norwich Union* (2000)). In other cases, even narrower submarkets have been identified. For example, private medical insurance, permanent health insurance, critical illness cover, long-term care insurance, health cash plans, dental benefit plans and income protection insurance are all complementary products in separate markets *within* health insurance.

The relevant geographic market for insurance and reinsurance products has been defined narrowly in the past as the national market in which the undertakings operate (*UAP/Provincial* (1994)).

What constitutes an abuse of a dominant position?

Insurance businesses with significant market shares must take care not to exploit their market power in an anti-competitive way. However, having a dominant position is not of itself unlawful – it is only the abuse of that position that is prohibited.

To be in a position of 'dominance', a business must have the ability to act independently of its customers, competitors and consumers (*Hoffman-La Roche (1979)*). This requires a complex assessment of a number of elements, including market definition, market shares, conditions of competition, entry barriers and buyer power. As a rule of thumb, a 40 to 50 per cent market share can be indicative of dominance.

The abuse by a business of its dominant position involves unilateral actions or practices rather than an agreement with another party. Examples of behaviour that could amount to an abuse include:

∎ unfair trading terms – imposing unfair purchase or selling prices or other trading conditions (e.g. exclusivity, excessive or predatory pricing);
∎ refusal to supply; and
∎ tying – requiring acceptance of unrelated supplementary obligations.

No exemptions are available where a business is abusing its dominant position. There may, though, in certain circumstances, be an objective justification for such behaviour and therefore no infringement of competition law.

How do the rules affect different types of distribution agreements?

I *Distribution agreements with non-competitors*

Agreements between underwriters and intermediaries for the distribution of insurance products may take a variety of forms: genuine and non-genuine agencies, brokerage, intermediation, distributorships, corporate partnerships and 'white labelling' (whereby one party's 'brand' is used for marketing). These arrangements are classified as 'vertical' agreements, that is, agreements between undertakings operating at different levels of the production or distribution chain. As mentioned earlier, intra-group agreements and agreements between a company and a genuine agent fall outside the scope of the competition rules. The rules do apply to vertical agreements but they do not generally give rise to serious competition concerns. Most have overriding benefits for markets and consumers (for example, opening up access to a market and thus promoting competition or improving efficient distribution). Any restrictions of competition contained in such agreements (for example, a grant of exclusivity) will often be ancillary to the overall purpose of the agreement. Of course, if the agreement contains no restrictions of competition at all, the competition rules will not apply.

Exemptions

There is no special exclusion from the competition rules for vertical agreements for the distribution of insurance or reinsurance products or services. However, where an agreement contains an appreciable restriction of competition, it may still benefit from one of three types of exemption – provided, that is, that the restriction does not constitute an abuse of a dominant position.

Agreements that may affect trade within the EU may be exempted under a 'block exemption' (i.e. a group exemption, which automatically exempts certain types of agreements falling within its terms). Agreements that may affect trade within the UK may be exempted under a 'parallel exemption' (i.e. an automatic exemption from the UK rules if an EU block exemption would otherwise apply at EU-level).

If an agreement does not fit squarely within a block exemption or parallel exemption, it is not automatically unlawful or unenforceable. This will only be the case if the agreement has an appreciable effect on competition. It will also be necessary to consider whether an agreement may be 'individually exempted' on the grounds that the restrictions of competition are outweighed by the benefits (*Article 81(3) of the EC Treaty* and *Section 9 of the Competition Act 1998*). Insurance businesses must self-assess whether their agreement meets the exemption criteria.

There are two relevant EC block exemptions that may apply to the distribution of insurance: the insurance block exemption and the vertical agreements block exemption. The latter provides a 'safe harbour' for distribution agreements between non-competitors, i.e. an automatic exemption from the competition rules so long as the underwriter's share of the relevant insurance market does not exceed 30 per cent and the agreement contains no hard core restrictions, e.g. resale price maintenance or market sharing (*Commission Regulation 2790/1999*). The exemption does not apply to agreements whose subject matter is dealt with by other EC block exemptions such as the insurance block exemption – for example, co-insurance arrangements (see Section III below). Eligibility for the vertical agreements block exemption depends on certain key factors. These are examined below.

Duration

If an exclusive agreement is for a minimum term that does not exceed five years (including any notice period for its termination), the non-compete restrictions in the agreement will usually be enforceable. Nevertheless, in certain circumstances the competition authorities might investigate whether the effect of the arrangement would be to restrict competition.

Exclusivity

If the parties are not actual or potential competitors (see below), the exclusivity restrictions during the term of the agreement will be enforceable unless the underwriter has more than 30 per cent of the relevant market.

Exclusivity in this context means that the parties agree not to act against each other's interests. The underwriter agrees not to enter into similar arrangements with any of the distributor's competitors or to market to the distributor's customers or any customer group reserved to it in its own right. It may also agree that where it offers better prices or terms and conditions to any of its customers it will offer the same (or better) to the distributor and/or their customers. By the same token, the distributor may agree not to appoint any other underwriter and not to offer, sell or promote any competing insurance product to its customers, nor to underwrite such a product itself. An exclusivity restriction that is capable of continuing beyond five years will only rarely be enforceable.

An exclusivity restriction imposed on either the underwriter or the intermediary or distributor post-termination will never be enforceable.

Pricing

Distributors must be able to determine freely the prices at which they supply insurance to their customers. There must be no restriction on the retail (gross) premium that they charge – this would be resale price maintenance, a form of price fixing that is regarded as a serious restriction of competition.

As a general rule, parties in corporate partnership agreements will be free to set, by agreement between them or at the discretion of either party, the net premium (according to a formula, if required), the commission retained by the distributor and the gross premium (and a profit sharing mechanism). However, there must never be any restriction on the distributor sharing its commission with the customer (for example, through a rebate, bonus etc).

Territories

Underwriters may allocate to distributors exclusive geographic territories (or customer groups) and prevent them from *actively* soliciting customers located in another distributor's exclusive territory. However, they cannot prevent 'passive selling' – whereby a distributor provides a quote to a customer based in another's exclusive territory at the customer's *unsolicited* request.

The underwriter may agree to refrain from selling directly to customers in distributors' exclusive territories (or they may reserve the right to do so or in relation to specific customers).

Dominance

Having a dominant position in the product market may prevent an underwriter from imposing exclusivity restrictions on a distributor (and may even prevent exclusivity restrictions being imposed on the underwriter). In addition, the underwriter may be subject to constraints for prices and other terms and conditions that it negotiates with the distributor. For example, it can be an abuse of a dominant position to differentiate between trading partners without objective justification. This may prevent an underwriter offering its larger distributors more favourable terms than smaller distributors.

II Distribution agreements with competitors

Co-operation between competitors is always viewed with suspicion; joint distribution by competitors is generally regarded as creating the potential for price collusion and market sharing. In any contacts with competitors, insurers should be careful not to enter into any agreement or concerted practice that has as its object or effect direct or indirect price fixing or resale price maintenance, the limit or control of production, markets, technical development or investment, and market or customer sharing.

Nevertheless, the insurance and (to a lesser degree) reinsurance markets have certain special characteristics that may permit certain types of co-operation, even in relation to joint distribution. Permitted co-operation is that which will have overriding benefits for consumers in the insurance market. For example, where risks are of a sufficient scale, rarity or novelty that they cannot be covered by one individual insurer (or reinsurer), it may in practice stimulate competition if insurers pool together and offer combined cover.

Actual or potential competitors

If the distributor and underwriter are actual or potential competitors, a distribution agreement between them would not automatically infringe competition law. However, it would need to be drafted very carefully. Certain terms – for example, pricing provisions and exclusivity restrictions – may be 'unsafe'. Specialist legal advice would need to be sought.

In determining whether the distributor is a potential competitor, it is necessary to consider whether it could and would be likely to enter the market for the product in question (either itself or through another group company) in response to a small and permanent increase in pricing.

Essentially, *the potential to compete* exists if:

■ the distributor is able to begin underwriting the product within a maximum of a year;
■ there is a realistic prospect of it actually doing so in response to a 5 to 10 per cent increase in prices for the product. (It is not necessary for the distributor to have stated its intention to enter the market – although such a statement might be taken as proof); and
■ the possibility of competition from the distributor acts as a constraint on the pricing strategy or other behaviour of those already in the market.

Exemptions

The EC vertical agreements block exemption does not generally apply to distribution agreements between actual or potential competitors. The exception is where the agreement is a *non-reciprocal* distribution agreement

– for example, where an underwriter becomes the distributor of the insurance products of another underwriter but the latter does not become the distributor of the products of the first underwriter.

A non-reciprocal agreement qualifies for the exemption if one of the following applies:

a) the distributor's total annual turnover does not exceed €100m;
b) the underwriter underwrites and distributes the insurance products, while the distributor only distributes them and does not underwrite competing products;
c) the underwriter is a provider of services at several levels of trade, while the distributor does not provide competing services at the level of trade where it purchases the products.

The EC insurance block exemption applies to certain agreements between 'rival' insurers provided that the co-operation does not go beyond what is justified by consumer interest and, in particular, does not concern policy cover, policy terms or premiums (*Commission Regulation 358/2003*). It covers the following types of agreements between competitors:

∎ joint calculations of the average cost of covering a specified risk;
∎ joint compilations of mortality tables, tables showing illness, accident and invalidity rates, and studies of the frequency or scale of future claims for given risks;
∎ the joint establishment of non-binding standard policy conditions for direct insurance;
∎ the joint establishment and management of insurance pools; and
∎ the joint testing and acceptance of security devices.

For the purposes of this publication, the most relevant category is the joint establishment and management of pools – the common coverage of certain types of risks by insurance groups i.e. co-insurance or co-reinsurance. The exemption applies if the insurance products underwritten within the arrangement do not have more than 20 per cent of the relevant market and the following conditions are met:

∎ each participating undertaking is able to withdraw from the group on not more than one year's notice, without any sanctions;
∎ there is no obligation on any member of the group to insure or reinsure through the group, in whole or in part, any risk of the type covered by the group;

- there is no restriction on the activity of the group or its members regarding the insurance or reinsurance of risks located in any particular geographical part of the EU;
- the agreement does not restrict output or sales;
- the agreement does not allocate markets or customers;
- the members of a co-reinsurance group do not agree on the commercial premiums they charge for direct insurance; and
- no member of the group is also a member of, or exercises a determining influence on the commercial policy of, a different group active in the same relevant market.

If the agreement fails to meet all the above conditions, it may still be permitted under the competition rules but would have to be assessed under the individual exemption criteria.

III Mergers and acquisitions

EU or national merger control rules will apply to situations where competing underwriters or competing intermediaries merge and there is a change of control. However, the rules may also apply where an underwriter acquires a distributor or intermediary – i.e. in cases of vertical integration.

The EU merger control rules apply to large-scale pan-European mergers. Notifications may be required (pursuant to *EU Merger Regulation 139/2004*) where, among other tests, the combined aggregate worldwide turnover of all the companies concerned (including the acquirer's group) exceeds a threshold of €2.5bn.

Where these thresholds are met, the EU merger control regime imposes mandatory notification requirements and requires the completion of a merger to be suspended until clearance has been granted by the European Commission.

In the UK (*Enterprise Act 2002*), merger thresholds will be met if the transaction creates or augments a market share (of demand or supply) of 25 per cent or more in the UK or a substantial part of it; or the value of the target's annual turnover in the UK exceeds £70m.

However, unlike some other national merger control regimes, there is no obligation to notify the merger to the OFT or to obtain clearance either before or following completion – filing in the UK is always voluntary. The OFT does, however, have the power to investigate a completed merger at any time up to four months after completion. If it concludes that there are substantive competition concerns, it is duty-bound to refer the case to the Competition Commission (CC) for an in-depth investigation.

Substantive competition issues generally arise only if there is an overlap between the activities of the merging parties in the relevant market and if the merger may be expected to 'substantially lessen competition' (UK test) or 'significantly impede effective competition' (EU test).

In vertical mergers, if intermediation and underwriting are considered as separate frames of reference, the parties will be active at two separate levels of the supply chain. Generally, harmful vertical effects are only likely where one of the merging parties has substantial power in a market in the supply chain. Therefore vertical mergers often do not give rise to substantive competition concerns.

The merger control rules may also apply where competing underwriters establish or become shareholders in a joint-venture vehicle for the distribution of insurance products. If the joint venture is established as an independent stand-alone entity operating at arm's length from its parents and jointly controlled by them, it may be considered to be a 'full-function' joint venture and may constitute a merger for the purposes of the EU merger control rules, thereby triggering a mandatory merger filing. In this case, certain conditions may be imposed that are similar to those required for business-to-business joint ventures: the aim will be to avoid the alliance being used as a vehicle for anti-competitive collusion and information exchange between the parent companies.

How do we ensure compliance?

In view of the serious penalties for breaches of competition law (see the box on page 142), it is important to promote an understanding inside the business of what is or is not allowed. One way to achieve this is by creating and actively implementing a competition compliance policy.

In the event of an investigation, the competition authorities are likely to look favourably on genuine attempts to stay within the law. In other words, being proactive could lead to a reduction in fines. It will also help to ensure that your distribution agreements are enforceable.

For a compliance programme to be effective, the company must be able to show that:

∎ there are appropriate policies and procedures in place;
∎ the programme has been effectively implemented;
∎ the programme has the visible and continuing support of, and is observed by, senior management;
∎ there is active and ongoing training for employees at all levels who may be involved in activities that are affected by competition law; and

■ the programme is evaluated, and formal audits are carried out at regular intervals to ensure that it is delivering its objectives.

If a company discovers that it has been party to an anti-competitive agreement, or is already the subject of an investigation, it is more likely to be dealt with leniently if it co-operates fully with the European Commission or the OFT. There is also the possibility for companies who have been parties to anti-competitive agreements to apply for leniency (effectively a form of whistle blowing) to the competition authorities and thereby secure complete immunity from, or a significant reduction in, penalties and, if applicable, criminal sanctions.

Enforcement of competition law

The European Commission is primarily responsible for enforcing EU competition law and the Office of Fair Trading (OFT) for enforcing UK competition law. However, the OFT also has the power to enforce the EU rules in the UK.

The EU and UK competition authorities have significant powers to investigate suspected anti-competitive behaviour (including entering and searching business premises with or without a warrant – so-called 'dawn raids').

The risks of being a party to an anti-competitive agreement or abusing a dominant position are very serious. The competition authorities may impose penalties of up to 10 per cent of a company's worldwide turnover. In the UK, individuals directly involved in serious anti-competitive behaviour (for example, price-fixing cartels) face the threat of criminal prosecution, which could lead to imprisonment for a maximum of 5 years and/or unlimited fines; directors may also be disqualified for up to 15 years.

In each case, the companies concerned may face lengthy investigations by the competition authorities, which will potentially disrupt their businesses and damage their reputations. In addition, infringements may result in actions for damages from third parties that have suffered loss as a result of anti-competitive behaviour.

Fines are more likely to be imposed if the agreement contains hard core restrictions of competition, including resale price maintenance and restrictions on passive sales. Where less serious breaches occur, especially in distribution and other vertical agreements, the risks are correspondingly lower. Nonetheless, they still have significant implications for business. In particular, key provisions in agreements may become void and unenforceable (e.g. territory, exclusivity, restrictions, provisions relating to pricing/premiums); in some cases, the whole agreement may be void.

Recent developments

EU sector inquiry into business insurance

The European Commission has the power to initiate general inquiries into sectors of the economy where it believes pricing structures or other practices mean that competition might be restricted or distorted. At the time of writing, the Commission is undertaking a sector inquiry into the market for the supply of business insurance in the EU and has published an interim report (January 2007).

The Commission has expressed its concern that 'in some areas of business insurance, competition may not be functioning as well as it could' and that the opportunities for cross-border competition could be greater.

The Commission is examining all types of business insurance and does not exclude from its investigation any particular insurance product or service – although specific examples of its stated targets include property and casualty insurance and reinsurance, and insurance and reinsurance intermediation.

The main findings so far of the Commission focused on:

- market fragmentation along national lines and excess profitability especially for SME business;
- long-term insurance contracts reducing competition;
- 'best terms and conditions' clauses in reinsurance contracts with direct insurers;
- exposure of some insurance intermediaries to conflicts of interest;
- lack of transparency of intermediaries' remunerations; and
- doubts about the justification for co-operation between insurers and the scope of the Insurance Block Exemption.

While the Commission does not have the power to impose sector-wide remedies, the results of the inquiry could form the basis for subsequent investigations by the Commission against individual companies under Articles 81 or 82 of the EC Treaty. National competition authorities could launch parallel investigations under domestic competition law.

Recent developments

UK market investigation of payment protection insurance

Like the EU, the UK competition authorities have powers to undertake market-wide investigations. Following a super-complaint by the

Consumers Advice Bureau, the OFT undertook a market study of payment protection insurance (PPI). It sought the views of the PPI industry, relevant trade associations and consumer organisations on how well the PPI market delivered choice and value to consumers. Its conclusion was that while PPI provided worthwhile cover for some people, the way it was sold impeded fair competition.

Key concerns included:

■ the difficulties faced by consumers in obtaining information about alternative suppliers;
■ the technical nature and/or lack of transparency of the information available to them;
■ the high costs or other barriers to entry for stand-alone PPI providers;
■ the wide degree of variation in pricing in the sector; and
■ the fact that gross profit margins appeared high.

The OFT has referred the market to the Competition Commission (CC) for an in-depth investigation (February 2007). The CC has a maximum of two years to publish a report. At the end of the investigation, the CC has a wide discretion to take action – and this may include price controls and divestments. It also has extensive powers to accept undertakings or make orders to remedy any detrimental effect on competition or consumers.

The CC has already expressed concerns about PPI in the context of its market investigation of store cards. The main concerns focused on the linking of PPI to credit, the costs of cover and a lack of transparency and information for consumers.

The Financial Services Authority is also co-operating with the OFT and the CC in relation to the investigation of the PPI market in the UK. It has called on PPI sellers and providers to take urgent action to ensure that their selling practices are in line with regulatory requirements.

Sources of further information

European Commission: http://ec.europa.eu/comm/competition
Office of Fair Trading: http://www.oft.gov.uk
Competition Commission: http://www.competition-commission.org.uk
Financial Services Authority: http://www.fsa.gov.uk

13

Transfer of insurance business

This chapter deals with the transfer of insurance business from one party to another. It is divided into three. The first part looks at the circumstances in which employment regulations apply. The second examines the statutory mechanism for transferring a portfolio of insurance business. The third looks at what happens when a corporate partner decides to change the underwriter behind its insurance products.

I   Employment law: TUPE

When a business or part of a business becomes the responsibility of someone else or there is a change in the provider of a service, its workers are likely to be protected under employment law. Put simply, the new party or 'transferee' takes employees and employee rights and liabilities with it.

The relevant UK legislation is known as TUPE – the Transfer of Undertakings (Protection of Employment) Regulations. The regulations, introduced in 1981, were amended in April 2006. A summary of their implications is given in the box on page 152. The most significant change made in 2006 was to provide for a new type of service provision change transfer. Other than in exceptional circumstances, the regulations can now apply whenever there is a change in the provider responsible for a particular service.

When does TUPE affect insurance business?

TUPE can apply in the following circumstances.

Sale of a business or part

Where there is a sale of a business (or part of a business) from insurance company 1 to insurance company 2, that sale taking place by way of a sale of assets rather than a sale of shares.

Intra-group transfer of a business or part

Where, within a group of companies, there is a transfer of a business or part to another group company – i.e. an internal transfer.

Contracting out/outsourcing

Where there is a change in the provider of a particular service. This happens on:

- first-stage contracting out/outsourcing, where a client first contracts with an external third party to provide a service;
- second-stage contracting out/outsourcing, where a client re-tenders and there is a change from service provider 1 to service provider 2; and
- in-sourcing, where a client that has previously used an external service provider brings a particular service back in-house.

What are the legal tests for TUPE?

Under TUPE there are two different types of transfer. Consequently, there are two different tests for working out whether TUPE applies.

Type A – case law/business transfer

The first type is where there is a *'transfer of an undertaking, business or part of an undertaking or business situated immediately before the transfer in the United Kingdom to another person where there is a transfer of an economic entity which retains its identity'*. This effectively creates a two-part test:

1. Is there an economic entity?
2. Is there a retention of business identity?

The regulations state that an economic entity means *'an organised grouping of resources which has the objective of pursuing an economic activity, whether or not that activity is central or auxiliary'*. In other words, an economic entity can amount to very little; an organised grouping of employees carrying out a particular service may be enough for the first part of the Type A test.

In establishing whether business identity is retained, case law makes clear that this is to be determined by looking at all surrounding factors, including:

- the type of undertaking or business concerned;
- whether the business's tangible assets, such as buildings and moveable property, have transferred;
- the value of the business's intangible assets, such as intellectual property (IP) rights at the time of transfer;
- whether or not the majority of employees transfer;
- whether or not customers are transferred; and
- the degree of similarity between the activities carried out before and after the transfer, and the period, if any, in which the activities are suspended.

It is also made clear that in applying the second part of the test no *one* of the above factors will necessarily decide the issue.

Type B – service provision change transfer

This was introduced by the 2006 regulations to remove uncertainty over whether TUPE should apply to second-stage contracting out/outsourcing. The intent is to ensure that TUPE will comprehensively apply to service provision changes.

The legal definition of a *'service provision change'* covers any contracting-out scenario – first-stage and second-stage contracting out and the taking back of a service in-house.

The requirements in order for there to be a service provision transfer when there is a service provision change are set out below:

1. *'An organised grouping of employees situated in the UK which has as its principal purpose the carrying out of the activities concerned on behalf of the client'.* (This requirement is intended to confine service provision change transfers to circumstances where the previous provider had in place an identifiable team essentially dedicated to the service.)
2. *'The client intends that the activities will, following the service provision change, be carried out by the new service provider, other than in connection with a single specific event or task of short-term duration.'* (In other words, there is no service provision change transfer where a client contracts with another party in relation to a one-off buying-in of services unless it is for a lengthy period.)

3. *'The activities concerned do not consist wholly or mainly of the supply of goods for the client's use.'* The intent here is to distinguish the provision of services from the provision of goods.

Are insurer/intermediary relationships affected by TUPE?

An insurance company may have contractual relationships with a number of intermediaries for the supply and sale of insurance products. TUPE is capable of applying on an insurer first entering into an arrangement with an intermediary and on an insurer's arrangement with a particular intermediary coming to an end.

Insurer and intermediary first enter into a contract

TUPE could apply, subject to the tests above, to transfer staff from either the insurer itself or a current intermediary to the new intermediary. Ordinarily, however, TUPE should not apply as the new intermediary will not be taking over an existing business or the provision of an existing service from the insurer or a current intermediary.

Contract between intermediary and insurer comes to an end

TUPE could apply, subject to the tests above, to transfer staff from the intermediary to the insurer itself or to a new intermediary. Once again ordinarily, however, TUPE should not apply as neither the insurer itself nor any new intermediary will be taking over an existing business or the provision of an existing service from the current intermediary.

Examples of the (relatively rare) circumstances in which TUPE might apply to transfer staff are given below.

Sole right to sell a particular product in particular territories

Where the current intermediary has the sole right to sell a particular insurance product or to sell that product in a particular territory, and the insurer makes equivalent arrangements with another intermediary, or brings the sales arrangements back in-house, there is likely to be: the necessary economic entity and retention of business identity for a Type A transfer; and the necessary service provision change, and there may be the necessary organised grouping of employees (to sell the product) for a Type B transfer.

Administration of policies sold by a previous intermediary

Where the first intermediary sells a particular insurance product, and the insurer enters into a contract with a new intermediary for the ongoing administration/run-off of policies sold by the first intermediary, there could be: a stable economic entity and the retention of business identity as required for a Type A transfer; and the necessary service provision change – administration of policies passes from intermediary 1 to intermediary 2 – and organised grouping of employees.

Consequently, as in point 1 on page 147, the tests for Type A and Type B transfers may be met.

How does TUPE affect partnering arrangements?

Partnering arrangements, whereby a corporate partner markets and sells branded insurance in association with an insurer that underwrites the products and handles claims, are increasingly common (see Chapter 5). TUPE will not apply where the corporate partner has not previously sold branded insurance products or branded insurance products of a particular type to its customer base as there can be no question of TUPE applying where a particular business/service first commences. TUPE can apply, however, when a corporate partner changes its partnering arrangements.

If, for example, Bank A markets and sells motor insurance products of Insurer 1 to its customers, branding that motor insurance as 'Bank A Motor Insurance', but then terminates the arrangement and contracts with Insurer 2 for the sale of the same product, branded in the same way, both tests might be met. In relation to a Type B transfer, the service provision change would be Insurer 2 taking over the service of underwriting and claims handling from Insurer 1.

How can we manage risk in relation to TUPE transfer?

As we've seen, TUPE can apply in several contexts – acquisitions, internal transfers, contracting out, insurer/intermediary partnering arrangements etc. Whatever the circumstances, the parties will probably wish to agree specific provision for the allocation of potential employee liabilities. This is normally done through the negotiation of express employment warranties and indemnities within the relevant contract.

The position is, of course, most straightforward in a business sale context, where there is a direct contractual relationship between party 1 and party 2 and where, therefore, indemnities and warranties are agreed between them.

Where there is no direct relationship, for example on a second-stage contracting-out where a second contractor takes on responsibility for a service from a first contractor, the transferee will generally need to seek any indemnity/warranty protection not from the transferor, the service provider it's taking over from, but from the client for which it will be providing the service. This means that a second contractor taking on responsibility for a service from a first contractor will seek indemnities from the client; and a new intermediary taking over the sale of a particular insurance product will seek indemnities from the insurer.

The types of provisions that will need to be sought are set out in broad terms below.

Provisions to protect the transferee

A transferee that will be immediately inheriting a workforce under TUPE should seek warranties confirming that:

- full details of all employment terms and conditions, benefits and policies have been disclosed;
- there has been full compliance with all appropriate employment legislation; and
- no employment claims are outstanding or expected on behalf of either employees themselves or their representatives.

In addition, a transferee should seek:

- a list of agreed 'transferring employees';
- an indemnity in respect of any differential between terms and conditions disclosed and terms and conditions on which transferring employees move;
- an indemnity for pre-transfer liabilities in relation to the transferring employees;
- an indemnity in relation to 'former employees' and 'retained employees' – former employees to cover the risk of claims from employees dismissed by the transfer for a reason connected to the transfer, liability for which will pass to the transferee, and retained employees to cover the risk of additional employees other than the agreed transferring employees transferring across; and
- an indemnity for failure to comply with collective obligations.

Provisions to protect the transferor

A transferor should seek:

- agreement that TUPE will apply to transfer staff;
- letters to relevant employees confirming that they have transferred by virtue of TUPE and that they are now employed by the transferee;
- an indemnity in respect of transferring employees post transfer;

- an indemnity with regard to collective obligations as a result of the transferee's failures; and
- an indemnity against any future claims from transferring employees.

Additional provisions – outsourcing and other service provision changes

A number of factors may necessitate the inclusion of additional indemnities when a contract is between a client and service provider in an outsourcing context. Many of them will also apply in the insurer/intermediary corporate partnering scenarios discussed previously. The main ones are as follows:

- the client will continue to be the recipient of the services of the transferring employees;
- the client may wish to ensure that the position of transferring employees or at least certain key employees is protected to ensure continuity of service;
- the client may wish to have some degree of involvement in or even veto over the recruitment of new employees to provide the service;
- the client will want to ensure that the contractor is not in a position to frustrate any future re-contracting out – or make provision of the service less attractive to other service providers; and
- the contractor may be concerned about being left with a 'parcel' of employee liabilities if it fails to secure the contract again and TUPE does not apply.

As a result of the above, a client in an outsourcing scenario may want to consider the following:

- a provision to protect transferring employees from detrimental changes to terms and conditions for a specified period or from dismissal;
- an obligation to provide 're-tendering information' on the employees then engaged in providing the service, backed up by an indemnity;
- a provision to prevent the contractor from increasing the remuneration of or otherwise improving the terms and conditions of employees then engaged in providing the service;
- a provision preventing the contractor from transferring employees in or out of the service; and
- an indemnity assignable to any replacement contractor against any employee liabilities before transfer.

A contractor may want to consider the following:

■ a requirement that the client makes it a condition of re-contracting out that the new contractor takes on the employees then engaged in providing the service;

■ an indemnity against redundancies in the event of a new contractor or the client not taking on the existing employees when the contract is terminated; and

■ an indemnity from the new contractor or the client against employee claims after re-transfer.

Provision of professional services

Application of Type B transfer rules

When a company changes the provider of a professional business service, for example legal advice, there will often be no implications under TUPE. As stated on page 147, a Type B transfer only occurs where the new arrangement is 'permanent' rather than ad hoc and the incumbent provider had in place an organised grouping of employees with the principal purpose of providing the service for the client. Although frequently providers of professional services such as legal services designate teams to service clients' accounts, they don't usually do so exclusively; the same employees will also work for other people. Hence, the requirements for a Type B transfer will not be fulfilled.

Summary of the implications of TUPE

When TUPE 'applies' there are implications for both transferor and transferee. These are briefly explained under the categories below.

Employees

Employees who were assigned to the business/service transfer to the new business/new service provider with their continuity of employment intact and on their existing contractual terms and conditions. (They have the right to refuse to transfer but, in normal circumstances, are unlikely to exercise it as it would amount to voluntary termination of their employment.)

Employee liabilities

Liabilities in relation to employees will also transfer. These could include, for example, liability for a failure to pay a bonus, liability for discrimination or personal injury.

Variations to contracts

Any variation of an employee's terms and conditions is void if the sole or principal reason for it is the TUPE transfer. Transfer-connected variations will only be legally effective in limited circumstances. It is therefore essential that employers wishing to make contractual changes seek detailed legal advice.

Dismissal

The dismissal of an employee is automatically unfair if the sole or principal reason for it is the transfer itself or a transfer-connected reason that does not constitute an economic, technical or organisational reason entailing changes in the workforce – i.e. 'an ETO reason'.

Where an ETO reason exists, ordinary unfair dismissal principles will apply and, therefore, dismissals could still be found to be unfair. Employers wishing to make dismissals, either before or after a TUPE transfer, should seek detailed legal advice.

Provision of information

One of the changes to TUPE introduced in April 2006 was to impose for the first time a stand-alone obligation on the transferor to provide specified information on employees to the transferee to ensure the new company or service provider is aware of the employment costs and any liabilities it will be inheriting.

Information and consultation with employee representatives

TUPE imposes detailed obligations to inform and consult appropriate representatives of staff who may be affected by the transfer. In the event of a failure to comply there is provision for a sanction of up to 13 weeks' pay per employee.

Collective agreements and trade union recognition

If the transferor recognised a trade union, so must the transferee. In the majority of cases, existing collective agreements with a trade union will apply as if made by or on behalf of the transferee.

II   Part VII transfers

The procedure for insurance business transfer schemes (often referred to as 'Part VII transfers') is set out in Part VII of FSMA (the Financial Services and Markets Act 2000). Part VII of FSMA provides the statutory process by which an insurer (the 'transferor') is able to transfer all or part of its insurance business to another insurer (the 'transferee').

Part VII of FSMA replaced the transfer process under Schedule 2C of the Insurance Companies Act 1982. Unlike Schedule 2C, FSMA requires transfers of **both** general and long-term business to be sanctioned by the court. The main relevant legal provisions can be found in:

- Part VII of, and Schedule 12 to, FSMA;
- the Financial Services and Markets Act 2000 (Control of Business Transfers) (Requirements on Applicants) Regulations 2001 (the 'Regulations'); and
- chapter 18 of the FSA Supervision Manual ('FSA Guidance').

An insurance business transfer scheme is defined in s.105 of FSMA. Broadly, the definition includes any scheme to transfer all or part of the insurance business of one insurer to another if:

a) the transferor is a UK authorised person and the business is being carried on in one or more EEA states; or
b) the business is reinsurance carried on in the UK by an EEA firm; or
c) the business is carried on by the transferor in the UK but the transferor is not a 'UK authorised person' or an EEA firm;

and in each case, following the transfer, the business will be carried on from an establishment of the transferee in the EEA.

Any transfer of insurance business which comes within the definition in s.105 FSMA (unless it is an excluded scheme) must be approved by the court.

Excluded schemes

Certain insurance business transfer schemes are specifically excluded from the requirement to comply with the procedure set out in Part VII. These include certain schemes relating to captive insurers and certain transfers of reinsurance business where, in either case, all affected policyholders have given their consent to the transfer. The parties to such schemes may (but do not need to) apply to the court to sanction the scheme.

Why undertake a Part VII transfer?

Part VII transfers can be used to transfer some or all of the insurance business of an insurer to another insurer; whether in the context of an intra-group reorganisation or, for example, the sale of an insurance business to a third party. They can also be used, in appropriate circumstances, in the context of demutualisations, fund restructurings and as an alternative to a scheme of arrangement. Some of the key features/benefits of a Part VII transfer are set out below:

■ The business transferred may include liabilities and potential liabilities under expired policies and/or current policies. The effect of a Part VII transfer is that the transferee becomes directly liable to policyholders under the transferring policies in respect of all such liabilities from the point the transfer becomes effective. Part VII transfers are often used as a means of achieving finality on a book of business in run-off, enabling the transferor to exit the market or a particular class of business and release regulatory capital. If the transferor has no other insurance business it may then be wound up.

■ Part VII allows the transferor to transfer its rights and obligations in respect of the transferring policies to the transferee without obtaining the express consent of the transferring policyholders.

■ The court has a wide discretion to transfer property and liabilities to the transferee and may make orders in relation to incidental, consequential and supplemental matters necessary to ensure the transfer is effectively carried out. The court may also make amendments to, or special provisions for, the benefits offered under the insurance contracts being transferred.

■ The court may transfer the benefit of reinsurance contracts which protect the transferring business without the express consent of reinsurers. This is a significant development from the previous Schedule 2C regime, which required consent from the relevant reinsurer in respect of every reinsurance contract (see 'What is the role of the court?' below).

■ Part VII allows business written at Lloyd's to be transferred to an insurance company. Although the provisions in FSMA only apply to current and certain former underwriting members (those who ceased underwriting after 24 December 2006), at the time of writing the Treasury proposes to remove this restriction so that all former Lloyd's names can participate in a Part VII transfer.

What is the role of the court?

Before sanctioning a Part VII transfer, the court will need to be satisfied that the requirements of FSMA have been fulfilled and it *'must consider that, in all the circumstances of the case, it is appropriate to sanction the scheme'* (s.111(3) FSMA). In determining whether it is appropriate to sanction the transfer, the court will take into account (among other things) the opinions of the FSA and the independent expert which must be appointed (see section 'What documents do you need?'). The FSA has the right to be heard at the court hearing, as does anyone who alleges they would be adversely affected by the proposed transfer.

As stated above, the court has a wide discretion under FSMA to transfer property and liabilities to the transferee. This discretion includes transferring property in certain circumstances where the insurer does not have the 'capacity' to make the transfer in question. There has been some uncertainty over the precise meaning of this provision in relation to reinsurance contracts which contain restrictions on transfer. However, at the time of writing the Treasury is consulting on changes to FSMA intended to remove this uncertainty and *'put beyond all doubt the ability of the courts to override contractual provisions that might otherwise have the effect of voiding or altering any contract subject to transfer'*. It is anticipated that the proposed changes will clarify that the court may transfer reinsurance contracts relating to the transferring business, including: (a) where the consent of the reinsurer has not been obtained; and (b) where the contract contains provisions restricting its transfer or purporting to terminate the contract upon any such transfer.

What is the role of the FSA?

The FSA is involved at various stages throughout the process. The FSA must approve the appointment of the independent expert and the form of his or her report (see 'What documents do you need?' below). Certain documents must be provided to, and approved by, the FSA. Before the court can sanction a transfer, certain certificates must be issued by the FSA – for example certifying that the transferee has (or will have) the necessary margin of solvency.

One of the FSA's regulatory objectives is the protection of consumers and this will be a key consideration for the FSA in the context of any transfer. The FSA is likely to object to a scheme if, in its view, it is unfair to a class of policyholders or if it concludes that the scheme has a material adverse effect on policyholders' security. The views of the FSA will in turn affect the court's decision whether or not to approve the scheme. Consequently, one of the first steps is to discuss the proposed transfer with the FSA. This will allow the regulator to consider what issues are likely to arise and allow a timetable to be agreed.

The FSA Guidance provides examples of factors it will consider when assessing the transfer. These include:

■ the purpose of the transfer;
■ how the security of policyholders' rights appears to be affected;
■ how the rights of others with an interest in the policies appear to be affected;
■ whether policyholders have been properly notified;
■ whether policyholders have been given adequate information and enough time to consider that information;
■ the opinion of the independent expert;
■ the views of other regulatory bodies; and
■ any views expressed by policyholders.

What are the requirements on applicants?

The court process involves an initial directions hearing, during which an order is sought on matters such as notification of policyholders. The Regulations set out the notification requirements, which include:

■ publication of notices in the UK press stating that an application for a Part VII transfer has been made to the court. Where an EEA country (other than the UK) is the state of commitment or the state in which the risk is situated, notices must also be published in two national newspapers in the relevant country; and
■ notifying all policyholders of the transferor and transferee of the proposed transfer.

Each of the requirements above may be waived by the court *'in such circumstances and subject to such conditions as the court considers appropriate'*. Reinsurers should, as far as possible, also be notified (see 'Notices to reinsurers' point 6 below).

After the notification process, a final court hearing before a judge is held in which the court may sanction the scheme. Detailed evidence in support of the application is usually provided by witness statement rather than in person. Once the court has sanctioned the scheme, office copies of the order must be delivered to the FSA and any final press notices in EEA states made (if applicable).

What documents do you need?

The key documents required for a Part VII transfer are listed below:

1. **Claim form and supporting witness statements.** The claim form is the official document used to make the application to the court. Witness statements are also submitted in support of the application.
2. **Independent expert's report.** An independent expert (normally an actuary) must be appointed by the parties to the transfer to provide a report on the proposed transfer. The expert must be approved by the FSA, and the report must be in a form that is FSA-approved. The independent expert's report is one of the most important documents in a Part VII transfer. It is required whether the transfer is of general or long-term insurance business. The main purpose of the report is to inform the court; it summarises the scheme and includes the expert's assessment of its likely effects on policyholders. The FSA will also place considerable reliance on the opinions contained in the independent expert's report in its assessment of the transfer.
3. **Actuary's report.** It is usual in transfers of long-term business for the actuarial function holder of each party (and, where the business includes with-profits policies, their with-profits actuaries) to prepare reports on the transfer. Such reports should be provided to the FSA and submitted to the court.
4. **Notices.** The press notices required (see 'What are the requirements on applicants?' above) must be approved by the FSA and then published in the UK press and, if applicable, national newspapers in other EEA states.
5. **Policyholder circular/explanatory statement.** A statement is sent to policyholders setting out the terms of the scheme and summarising the independent expert's report. This statement and summary, together with the independent expert's report, must be given to any person who asks for them.
6. **Notices to reinsurers.** Although currently the FSA expects to be informed of steps taken to consult with, or seek the consent of, reinsurers,

there is no statutory requirement to do so. The Treasury is currently consulting on changing this and imposing a specific requirement to notify reinsurers subject to any waiver granted by the court.

7. **Sale and purchase/business transfer agreement.** Often the parties to a Part VII transfer will enter into a separate agreement whereby the transferor agrees to sell or transfer the relevant business to the transferee. It may deal with the transfer of other assets and liabilities and include, for example, provisions dealing with matters relating to employees, associated contracts, IT systems, customer data and real property.

8. **Scheme document.** This is the underlying legal document that details the terms of the proposed transfer of the insurance business.

How long will the process take?

An important consideration for the timetable is whether the FSA will need to consult regulatory authorities in other EEA states, for example where the business being transferred includes business carried on in a branch in another EEA state or contracts for which the state of risk or state of commitment is another EEA state. As a general guide, around six months should be allowed to complete the preparation of the documents and the court process, although a straightforward scheme with no requirement to consult with, or obtain the consent of, overseas regulators may be completed more quickly. In more complicated cases and where overseas regulators must be notified or consulted, the process will often take longer. To avoid any unnecessary delay or expense, it is important to plan a Part VII transfer from the outset and to project manage it properly as it progresses.

III   Block transfer on renewal

It is not unusual for a corporate partner to change the insurance provider behind its insurance distribution arrangements. In these circumstances, responsibility for offering policy renewals passes from one insurer to another, and the contract with the customer changes. This section looks at the legal implications.

What's the relevant rule?

In the interests of consumer protection, the supply of unsolicited insurance services is restricted. Rule 4.7.1 of the FSA's Insurance: Conduct of

Business sourcebook (ICOB) requires that an insurance intermediary or an insurer must not: *'(a) supply a service to a retail customer without a prior request on his part, when the supply of such service includes a request for immediate or deferred payment'*; or *'(b) enforce any obligation against a retail customer in the event of unsolicited supplies of such services, the absence of reply not constituting consent.'*

This restriction applies to insurance intermediaries and insurers who, broadly, provide general insurance policies in circumstances where they are not face-to-face with the customer at the point of sale. It does not, however, apply to the tacit renewal of an insurance policy (ICOB 4.7.2 R). A tacit renewal is one where the insurer already has the right to renew without requiring any further request from the customer prior to renewal.

What does the rule mean?

When a partner decides to change the identity of its underlying insurer with effect from renewal, insurance policies provided by the incoming insurer will be new policies rather than renewals (because the parties to the contract of insurance are different). However, the partner is likely to want the provision of insurance to its customers to continue as if the policies were being renewed and any premiums to continue to be paid automatically. It will be keen to ensure that the change of insurer does not adversely affect its customer relationships and, in particular, will want to avoid any unnecessary communications with customers to obtain 'prior requests' as these will be both costly and potentially disruptive.

The effect of ICOB 4.7.1 R is that both the partner and the incoming insurer must ensure that they have obtained customers' prior requests before new insurance policies are provided.

It is, however, not completely clear what will constitute a prior request. It initially seemed that the FSA expected firms to obtain a *positive* request from customers, an FSA circular letter to insurers seems to accept that an *implied* request will be sufficient. The FSA letter is not official guidance but it does indicate the regulator's likely approach to the issue.

The way partners and insurers communicate with customers is likely to be decisive. People must be made fully aware of the circumstances in which an implied request will be taken to have been made.

New customers

At the point of selling policies, partners and insurers should consider obtaining the customer's agreement to any future transfer of the policy to another insurer. In order to achieve this, the FSA suggests (in its circular letter) that the possibility of such future transfers should be clearly drawn to the attention of any potential new customer and be given suitable prominence in agreements with customers going forward.

Existing customers

Partners and incoming insurers will need to contact existing customers to obtain 'prior requests' if they don't already have them. One approach suggested by the FSA in its letter is to send a terms of business agreement that:

■ includes a clause to the effect that before the end of any contract period, the customer will be advised on what terms a policy for a further period will be offered by the insurer of the current policy, or if the policy is no longer offered, the terms of any policy offered by another insurer; and

■ makes clear that the clause represents the customer's prior request for the firm to provide such a policy unless the customer indicates to the contrary; and that the customer has the option to revoke such a prior request.

In accordance with the provisions of ICOB and the FSA's Principles for Businesses, any such communications with customers will need to be clear, fair and not misleading about the prior request, its consequences and the option to revoke it.

Partners and insurers should also ensure that they have any other necessary authorities from customers. For example, customers' consent will be required, in accordance with data protection legislation, for the transfer of their personal data to the new insurer. Customers may also need to be contacted in connection with the bulk changing of any direct debit instructions in favour of the incoming insurer.

Index

abuse of dominant market position 134–35
advance payments to intermediaries 86–87
'advice giving' clauses, agency agreements 74
advising and selling standards 35–38
affinity arrangements *see* secondary insurance market
'agency by estoppel' concept 72
agency principles 6, 12, 68–79, 92–93, 94–95
   definition of 'agent' 68–69
   key issues in agency agreements 74–77
   rights and obligations 69–74, 85
appointed representatives (ARs) 18–19, 30, 56–57
'appreciable effect' 133
Approved Persons regime 25–28
Association of British Travel Agents (ABTA) 50–52
authority span of agents 71–74
authorised firms, breaches of rules 17–18

bank account management 97, 100–01, 101–03
block exemptions, competition rules 136, 138–40
block transfers on renewal 159–61
Bolam test 70
borderline cases 5, 63–65
brands 3, 128–30
breaches of regulations 16–18, 60–67
Business Standards section, FSA Handbook 15, 27, 28
buying trends 4
'by way of business' test 14–15

call centre outsourcing 106
cancellation rules 40–42, 46, 117–18
claims handling outsourcing 106–07
claims handling rules 42–44
claims management activities 55–56
Client Assets Sourcebook Chapter 5 (CASS 5) 93–94, 99
client funds 6, 92–103
   bank accounts for 101–03
   explanation of the rules 94–101
'collection of premiums' processes 83–84
collective agreements, TUPE regulations 154
co-mingling of funds 99–100
commercial and retail customers, ICOB Rules compared 36–46
commission rules 38, 85–86
common law duties of agents 70
communications rules 31, 33–34
'competition' influence on pricing 81–82
competition law 7, 131–44
   effect on different types of agreements 132–41
   enforcement 141–42
competitors, distribution arrangements with 138–40
Conduct of Business (COB) rules 10, 15, 28, 29, 47
connected contracts 15, 41–42, 50–53
Contracts (Rights of Third Parties) Act 77
controlled functions (CFs) 26
cooling off periods 40–42, 46, 117–18
'corporate partnership' arrangements 49, 78–79

credit risk transfer 92–95
criminal liability 16–17, 18

data protection 109, 122–28
data sharing 125–28
'demands and needs' statements 38
Disability Discrimination Act 118
disaster recovery schemes 64–65
disclosure requirements 37–38, 39–40,
    45–46, 82, 85
discretionary schemes 63
dismissals, TUPE regulations 153
distance contracts 39–40, 45–46, 84, 117–18
Distance Marketing Regulations 84, 117–18
domain names 129–30
due diligence process 56

e-commerce 116–22
Electronic Commerce (EC Directive)
    Regulations 116–17
Electronic Communications Act 117
Electronic Signatures Regulations 117
employee liabilities, TUPE regulations 153
employee representatives, TUPE regulations
    153
employment law, business transfers 7, 145–54
'enabling parties to communicate' exclusion
    54–55
EU sector inquiry into business insurance 143
'excessive charges' rule 32
exemptions
    competition law 135–37, 138–40
    ICOB rules 31, 35
exit management 113
express terms, agency agreements 69–70
extended warranty cover 52–53

fees disclosure 37
fees of intermediaries 90–91
fiduciary duties of agents 71, 85
financial promotion rules 11, 33–35
Financial Services and Markets Act (FSMA)
    2, 8–9, 10, 20–21
    breaches 16–18
    Part VII transfers 154–59
Financial Services Authority (FSA) 2–3,
    8–10, 20–21
    basic regulation framework 10–19
    general rules for regulated firms 20–28
    outsourcing rules 107–09
    Part VII transfers 156–57
    see also Insurance Conduct of Business
        Rules
fitness test (FIT) 26
fixed and floating charges 100

foreign insurers 5, 65–66
funds held by intermediaries 92–103

'general prohibition' 10, 11
governance rules 25–27, 112–13
Great Western case 65–66

Handbook, FSA 10, 20–28
Handbook Guides 28
High Level Standards block, FSA Handbook
    21–28

identity verification, online selling 121–22
implied terms, agency agreements 70–71
inadvertent breaches of the law 60–67
'incidental provision of information' exclusion
    53–54
information provision, TUPE 153
insolvency issues 97–99
Insurance Conduct of Business (ICOB) rules
    5, 15, 29–47, 159–60
'insurance' definition 5, 60–62
Insurance Premium Tax (IPT) 80, 84, 91
intermediaries 12–14, 44, 45–46, 119–21,
    148–49
    funds held by 92–104
    remuneration 85–91
    see also agency principles; secondary
        insurance market
internal systems and controls 25
introducer ARs 56, 57

joint venture rules 141

letters of credit 100

market definitions, competition law 134
'market practice' indicators, agency
    relationships 71–74
marketing factors in pricing decisions 82
material outsourcing arrangements 108
mediation activities, regulation of 12–14
Medical Defence Union Ltd v Department of
    Trade 63
mergers and acquisitions rules 140–42
Mortgage Conduct of Business (MCOB) rules
    47

National Insurance & Guarantee Corporation
    case 70
non-distance contracts, product disclosure 39
non-insurance organisations see secondary
    insurance market
non-motor goods, connected contracts
    52–53

on-demand bonds 100
online brands 128–30
online selling and servicing 116–22
Origo Standards 120
outsourcing 6, 104–15
    regulatory and legal implications 107–09
    transfers of business 146, 151–52
    trends and developments 105–07

parent company guarantees 101
Part VII transfers 154–59
partnering arrangements *see* secondary
        insurance market
'payment' element of insurance arrangement
        61, 62
payment of intermediaries *see* remuneration
'payment protection insurance' investigation
        143–44
'personal recommendation' rules 38
policy administration outsourcing 107
premiums, receiving and refunding 83–85
pricing of insurance products 80–83, 137
primary pooling 97–98
principal, agents acting for more than one 76
Principles, FSA 21–23
Privacy and Electronic Communications
        Regulations 118, 124
product disclosure rules 39–40
product trends 3–4
professional services, business transfer rules
        152
profit sharing 87–90
profitability factors in pricing decisions 82
'promise' element of insurance arrangements
        61–62
promotions, funding of 83
Prudential Standards and Sourcebook 28, 66

refunds 84–85
Regulated Activities Order (RAO) 10–11,
        12–14, 15, 50–56
regulations overview 2–3, 5, 8–19
Regulatory Guides and Processes, FSA
        Handbook 28
reinsurance mediation 99
remuneration of intermediaries 6, 75, 85–91
renewals rules 14
retail and commercial customers, ICOB Rules
        compared 36–46
risk management
    agency relationships 77–78
    e-commerce 118–19
    funds held by intermediaries 92–101
    TUPE transfers 149–51

'secondary' insurance market 2, 5, 48–59, 149
    appointed representatives 56–57
    contract principles 58–59
    regulation and exclusions 50–56
secondary pooling 98
selling online 116–22
selling and advising standards 35–38
Senior Management Arrangements, Systems
        and Controls (SYSC) module, FSA
        Handbook 25
service provision change transfers 147–48,
        152
servicing, online 120–21
standby letters of credit 100
Statement of Principles for Approved Persons
        (APER) 26
'status disclosure' rules 36–37
sub-agents 76–77
supervision manual (SUP), FSA Handbook 23
Supply of Extended Warranties Order 53

tax investigation schemes 64
technology, use of new 1–2, 7, 116–30
    selling and servicing 116–22
    use of personal data 122–28
third-party claimants, rules for 43–44
'third-party processor' rules 30, 37
trade marks 128–29
trade union recognition, TUPE regulations
        154
Training and Competence (TC) Rules 27
transfer of insurance business 7, 145–61
    block transfers 159–61
    employment law 110, 145–54
    Part VII transfers 154–59
Transfer of Undertakings (TUPE) Regulations
        110, 145–54
travel insurance, connected contracts 50–52
trusts 96–97, 101

unauthorised firms, breaches of rules 16–17
'uncertain event' element of insurance
        arrangement 61, 62
'unfair inducements' rule 31–32, 87
Unfair Terms in Consumer Contracts
        Regulations 84
'unsolicited services' restrictions 46

Value Added Tax (VAT) 87, 91, 115
variations to contracts, TUPE regulations 153
'vertical' agreements, competition rules
        135–37

warranties 52–53, 63–64